Glossary of Thoroughbred Racing

By Frank M. Briggs, Sr.

Including over eleven hundred terms used
around the race track.

Big House Publishing Co.

GLOSSARY OF THOROUGHBRED RACING

by Frank M. Briggs, Sr.

Published by:
Big House Publishing Co.
P.O. Box 202
Steger, IL 60475

Library of Congress Cataloging-in-Publication Data

Briggs, Frank M., 1944–
   Glossary of throughbred racing.

   1. Horse-racing--Terminology.
   2. Horse race betting--Terminology.
   3. Thoroughbred horse--Terminology.
I. Title.
SF321.5.B75 1987   798.4'3'014   86–70592
ISBN 0–937529–04–4
ISBN 0–937529–03–6 (soft)

ABOUT THE AUTHOR

Frank Briggs Sr. lives with his family on a small horse farm near Chicago Hts., IL. He is involved in breeding, breaking and training of Thoroughbred horses. He is married and has three sons. His wife Charlene owns and races a few horses on the Chicago circuit.

His oldest son Frank Jr. is currently one of the leading jockeys in the Chicago area. He is a very popular young man known for his ability and desire to win. His son Edward, who wants to become a trainer, gallops and grooms horses on the farm. His youngest son Robert who hopes to become a Veterinarian also helps take care of horses on the farm.

Frank Briggs Sr. has spent over five years compiling the information for his book. He has devoted a great deal of time and effort to insure that this book is a big aid to people interested in Thoroughbred Horse Racing.

IN APPRECIATION

I want to thank my family and friends who helped throughout the difficult times while I was compiling the information for this book. Also my thanks to everyone who helped me go over the many details necessary to produce this book. My thanks also to the Daily Racing Form who gave me permission to reprint many articles.

CONTENTS   Page

INTRODUCTION

In this book you will find a tremendous amount of information regarding Thoroughbred Horse Racing. You will learn many racing terms and definitions that you may have heard but never understood. This book is a must for anyone interested in Thoroughbred Horse Racing, from the person who is making his first trip to the track, to someone already working on the backside. Each should be knowledgeable of the terms pertaining to racing. This book includes over eleven hundred terms used in and around racing. It also includes information designed to aid people who could be coming to the track for the first time, and also to help some of the more experienced horse players brush up on the basics of betting. I'm sure you will find this book interesting, educational, and informative. I know this book will be a big aid to increasing your knowledge of Thoroughbred Horse Racing.

Good Luck and Good Racing

FRANK BRIGGS, SR.

WELCOME TO THE WORLD OF RACING

Horse racing, considered the top spectator sport in the United States for many years, has an annual attendance that exceeds that of any major league sports including baseball, football, basketball, etc.

This is largely due to pari-mutual wagering that is allowed in horse racing.

Horse racing is one of the few sports where the spectator is legally able to place wagers on the outcome of each race.

There is also a certain excitement in watching a horse race and hoping your horse wins. A person picks a horse to win for many reasons. Some are good, some are bad, some are right and some are wrong. For whatever reason a person picks a horse, that person soon finds out whether it was the right decision or not. There is no need to wait weeks, months, or years to find out. A race doesn't take long. In a matter of minutes a person can see what kind of decision was made. If you picked a winner, you'll be jumping for joy. If not you'll be disappointed. No one person can pick all winners; anything can happen in a horse race.

The main thing is to have an enjoyable day at the races and hopefully return home a winner. At the track, you will be able to enjoy dinner and cocktails or if you prefer there are many refreshment stands with an assortment of various foods.

You will have your choice of going to the Club House, which is considered more exclusive, or remain in the grandstand areas. There is an additional fee to go into the Club House.

Located around both the grandstand area and the Club House, are TV monitors which show a multitude of betting information and a close-up view of the race. After each race is declared official, the race is re-run on the TV monitor.

Whether you watch the race from the TV monitor, the Club House, or the grandstand, you will find the excitement of the crowd and the thrill of the race, something you will never forget.

BASICS OF BETTING

It is every horseplayer's dream to consistently win at the races. This is a dream that does not often come true. It takes a lot of luck, patience, and figuring, to come out a winner. Understanding how to bet, and how to make an educated decision in picking a horse, will surely help.

Every day, at race tracks all over the world there are thousands of dollars in winning tickets thrown away. Many of these tickets are discarded because the bettor did not realize that they were holding a winning ticket. Many other tickets are thrown away or destroyed before the race is declared "Official". A race is not declared official until all the riders have dismounted and check in. If the jockeys' weights are correct and there is no official inquiry or any other claims of foul, the official sign is posted on the tote board. If an inquiry is lodged, and the stewards uphold the claim of foul, the winning horse could be disqualified and another horse declared the winner. Everyone who bets on the horse that was finally declared the winner and had already discarded or destroyed their tickets, would have been out of luck.

This is why it is so important not to destroy or throw away your tickets, until the race has been declared official. Many tickets are thrown away because the bettor doesn't understand the basics of betting. When placing a bet on a horse, you can bet it to WIN, PLACE, or SHOW.

WIN — When you bet a horse to win, you are betting that the horse will finish the race in first place. The horse must win the race in order for you to collect your bet. Generally the payoff is larger than on a place or show bet.

PLACE — When you bet a horse to place, you are betting the horse will finish at least in second place. The horse must either win the race or finish in second place for you to collect your bet. Generally the payoff is larger than on a show bet.

SHOW — When you bet a horse to show, you are betting that the horse will come in at least in third place. The horse must finish the race in first, second or third place for you to collect your bet.

There are many tickets discarded by people who bet on a horse to place or show and do not realize they are entitled to collect on these bets if the horse wins the race. This may seem elementary to you, but you would be surprised how many people just don't know.

When you bet a horse "across the board", it means that you are betting an equal amount of money to Win, Place, and Show. At some tracks where they don't have the most modern "totalizator" system, they may sell combination tickets. A six dollar combination ticket would be the same as betting $2.00 to Win, $2.00 to Place, and $2.00 to Show.

A combination ticket has cash value and can be cashed if the horse that was bet, finished in the money, which means the horse finished first, second, or third, in the race.

There is also a lot of confusion for the beginning bettors, that involves "gimmick" races, on which you bet a combination of horses.

DAILY DOUBLE — A wager where you must select the winners of two successive races. Both of the horses you select must win their respective race. There are no PLACE or SHOW bets involved in Daily Double wagering. Daily Double wagering is usually on the first two races on the program: although some tracks have two Daily Double Pools.

QUINELLA — A wager where you must select the first two horses to cross the finish line, regardless of the order in which they finish the race.

PERFECTA or EXACTA — A wager where a bettor must name the first and second place horses, in the exact order of finish, to win.

TRI-FECTA — A race where the bettor must pick the first, second and third place horses, in the exact order of finish to win.

BIG SIX - SWEEP SIX - PIC SIX — A wager where you must select the winners of six successive races.

There are also other "gimmick" races, such as the Double Perfecta, Twin Exacta, or the Twin Double, that are combinations of the races we have already discussed. These types of wagers are not used as frequently as the gimmick races we have discussed. Normally, the rules for these races are listed in the Official Program.

The pay-off for each gimmick race is not determined by what is bet on each horse in the regular betting pools. Each of the gimmick races has a separate betting pool. The odds on the tote board do not reflect the odds or money bet on the gimmick race. The odds for the gimmick races and the probable pay-offs are sometimes displayed on closed circuit TV monitors, during the betting period, before each gimmick race.

Quite often, there will be both Quinella and Perfecta Wagering on the same race. The second race on the program, which is usually the second half of the Daily Double, also normally, has Quinella Wagering. The Official Program will tell you what types of wagering will be on each race.

If you are starting to get confused by the various types of wagers, just keep in mind, that you don't have to bet all the races, and on all the gimmick races to have a good time at the race track. You can just bet to Win, Place, or Show, or a combination of these. Keep in mind a gimmick race is just that, **A Gimmick Race.**

Most of the people going to the track love the gimmick races because of the larger pay-offs. Keep in mind, the reason the pay-offs are larger is because the winners are harder to select. Unless you understand how to bet these races and what is required to win, it can turn out to be a losing proposition for you. It may also turn out to be the same old story of throwing your money away by throwing the winning ticket away because you didn't realize it was a winner. So, before betting the races, be sure you know and understand the rules.

The Official Program is usually the first thing you purchase as you enter the race track. The Program lists the horses in each race and the position in which they are to start the race. The number one post position is the position closest

14

to the inside rail. In the Program you will also find horses listed as an Entry. An Entry is two or more horses owned or trained by the same person, racing as a unit in the betting. A bet on an Entry will pay-off if either one of those horses finishes in the position wagered. Along with the post position and the name of the horse, the Program lists the owner, trainer, the jockey, the weight the horse is assigned to carry, which includes the jockey, and the probable odds at which the horse is expected to race.

The Program also has a multitude of information including: jockey standings, trainer standings, conditions of the race, the color of the silks the jockey will wear, information on the race course, information on the management of the track, how to wager on different gimmick races and more.

A Program is a must for anyone going to the track.

The Program can also be a big aid to the beginning bettor in making selections. An expert established the probable odds listed in the Program. These odds that are listed in the program are the odds that the horses are expected to go off at. It does not necessarily mean that the horses will go off at these odds, or that the horse with the lowest odds will actually win the race. As you may well know, the experts are not always correct. Based on these odds, you will be able to determine in what order the experts think the horses will finish.

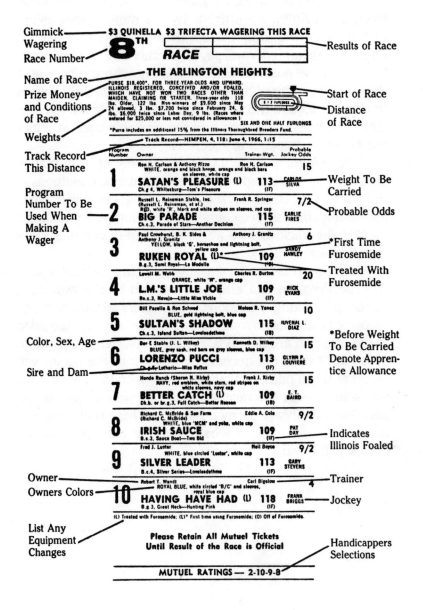

Gimmick → **$3 QUINELLA $3 TRIFECTA WAGERING THIS RACE**

Wagering

Race Number → **8**TH

RACE ← Results of Race

Name of Race → **THE ARLINGTON HEIGHTS**

Prize Money and Conditions of Race →

PURSE $18,400*. FOR THREE-YEAR-OLDS AND UPWARD. ILLINOIS REGISTERED, CONCEIVED AND/OR FOALED, WHICH HAVE NOT WON TWO RACES OTHER THAN MAIDEN, CLAIMING OR STARTER. Three-year olds 118 lbs. Older, 122 lbs. Non-winners of $9,600 since May 24 allowed, 3 lbs. $7,200 twice since February 24, 6 lbs. $6,000 twice since Labor Day, 9 lbs. (Races where entered for $25,000 or less not considered in allowances.)

← Start of Race

← Distance of Race

SIX AND ONE HALF FURLONGS

*Purse includes an additional 15% from the Illinois Thoroughbred Breeders Fund.

Weights →

Track Record This Distance → Track Record—HEMPEN, 4, 118; June 4, 1966, 1:15

Program Number	Owner	Trainer-Wgt.	Probable Jockey Odds
1	Ron H. Carlson & Anthony Rizzo WHITE, orange and black hoops, orange and black bars on sleeves, white cap **SATAN'S PLEASURE (L)** Ch.g 4, Whitesburg—Tom's Pleasure	Ron H. Carlson 113 CARLOS SILVA (IF)	15
2	Russell L. Reineman Stable, Inc. (Russell L. Reineman, et al.) RED, white 'R', black and white stripes on sleeves, red cap **BIG PARADE** Ch.c.3, Parade of Stars—Another Decision	Frank R. Springer 115 EARLIE FIRES (IF)	7/2
3	Paul Crowhurst, B. K. Sides & Anthony J. Granitz YELLOW, black 'G', horseshoe and lightning bolt, yellow cap **RUKEN ROYAL (L)*** B.g.3, Semi Royal—La Modelle	Anthony J. Granitz 109 SANDY HAWLEY (*B)	6
4	Lowell M. Webb ORANGE, white 'W', orange cap **L.M.'S LITTLE JOE** Ro.c.3, Navajo—Little Miss Vickie	Charles R. Burton 109 RICK EVANS (IF)	20
5	Bill Pacella & Ron Schwed BLUE, gold lightning bolt, blue cap **SULTAN'S SHADOW** Ch.c.3, Island Sultan—Loveleadethme	Moises R. Yanez 115 JUVENAL L. DIAZ (IB)	10
6	Bar-E Stable (J. L. Wilkey) BLUE, grey sash, red bars on grey sleeves, blue cap **LORENZO PUCCI** Ch.g.4, Lothario—Miss Reflux	Kenneth D. Wilkey 113 GLYNN P. LOUVIERE (IF)	15
7	Honda Ranch (Sharon N. Kirby) NAVY, red emblem, white stars, red stripes on white sleeves, navy cap **BETTER CATCH (L)** Dk.b. or br.g.3, Full Catch—Better Reason	Frank J. Kirby 109 E. T. BAIRD (IB)	15
8	Richard C. McBride & Son Farm (Richard C. McBride) WHITE, blue 'MCM' and yoke, white cap **IRISH SAUCE** B.c.3, Sauce Boat—Two Bid	Eddie A. Cole 109 PAT DAY (IF)	9/2
9	Fred J. Lutter WHITE, blue circled 'Lutter', white cap **SILVER LEADER** B.c.4, Silver Series—Loveleadethme	Neil Boyce 113 GARY STEVENS (IF)	9/2
10	Robert T. Wendt ROYAL BLUE, white circled 'B/C' and sleeves, royal blue cap **HAVING HAVE HAD (L)** B.g.3, Great Neck—Hunting Pink	Carl Bigelow 118 FRANK BRIGGS (IF)	4

(L) Treated with Furosemide; (L)* First time using Furosemide; (O) Off of Furosemide.

Program Number To Be Used When Making A Wager →

Weight To Be Carried →

Probable Odds →

*First Time Furosemide →

Treated With Furosemide →

Color, Sex, Age →

Sire and Dam →

*Before Weight To Be Carried Denote Apprentice Allowance

Indicates Illinois Foaled →

Owner →

Owners Colors →

Trainer ←

Jockey ←

List Any Equipment Changes →

Please Retain All Mutuel Tickets Until Result of the Race is Official

Handicappers Selections →

MUTUEL RATINGS — 2-10-9-8

16

There are other experts beside those making the selections for the Program. Most newspapers, including the Daily Racing Form, have handicappers that make selections for them. Also professional handicappers sell their racing selections in the form of "tip sheets" which are usually sold at the entrance to most race tracks. Some of these handicappers are excellent, while others are only mediocre. If you don't know anything about handicapping a horse race, then it is undoubtedly better to make a selection based on a handicappers selection, as in the Racing Form or a tip sheet, than selecting a horse at random, or by the name, or the color of the horse, or some other similar method.

If you want to try your hand at handicapping or learn about the horse you plan to bet on, you must read the Daily Racing Form. The Racing Form shows the past performance record of all the horses in the Program along with the latest workouts, and other information to aid you with your selection. You cannot handicap or make a proper selection without it. Like the Program, you can purchase the Racing Form at the entrance of the track, or you can do as many others do, and purchase it the night before at your favorite newstand. That way you will have plenty of time to study it before going to the races. In the next chapter we will discuss how to read the Racing Form.

Understanding the odds is sometimes difficult for the beginning bettor. The odds on the tote board are determined by the bettors. Pari-Mutuel betting is actually betting against each other. People are sometimes under the misconception that the race track makes the odds and that they are betting against the race track. This is not true. The race track merely acts as a broker. The race track, and the State that the race track is in receive a percentage of all the money that is bet on each race. The cut or percentage taken out from the money bet on each race is approximately 15 to 18% on regular races and as high as 25% on gimmick races. The revenue generated to state governments by racing has reached as high as 700 Million Dollars per year. This revenue helps to reduce taxes, and finances many state projects. It is because of this revenue that many states have pari-mutuel racing and many more are in the process of starting it. Since the State and the track take their cut or commissions out of each race, it makes no difference to them if a favorite or a long-shot wins the race.

The odds against each horse, and the eventual pay-off figures are determined by the people placing the bets. The more money that is bet on a certain horse, the smaller the return if the horse wins. The entire win pool, minus the cut by the States and the track, must be divided by the holders of winning tickets. The more money that is bet on the winner, the less the ticket holders receive per dollar bet. If a longshot wins the race which means relatively few people placed wagers on that particular horse, then they divide the entire win pool, minus the cut, and therefore get a lot more money back per dollar wagered than the person betting on the favorite when it wins.

APPROXIMATE PAY-OFF FOR
A $2.00 WIN TICKET

ODDS	PAY-OFF
1-9	$2.20
1-5	2.40
2-5	2.80
3-5	3.20
4-5	3.60
1-1	4.00
6-5	4.40
7-5	4.80
3-2	5.00
8-5	5.20
9-5	5.60
2-1	6.00
5-2	7.00
3-1	8.00
4-1	10.00
5-1	12.00
6-1	14.00
7-1	16.00

There are separate pools for Place and Show bets. When betting to Place or Show, the pay-off is determined by first dividing the pool into two parts in the case of the Place pool, and in three parts in the Show pool, and then dividing these parts among the holders of the appropriate tickets on the horses involved. Keep in mind that the State and track get their cuts before any divisions of the pools are made.

When you are considering how to bet a horse, it is important to realize that the horse that is considered the best horse in the race, has a better chance of finishing the race in second or third place, than it does winning the race. But since the profit on a successful Place or Show bet is realitively small in comparison to a Win bet, many people prefer to bet the horse to Win.

When you are figuring the odds and trying to determine the pay-off price on a horse, keep in mind that all pay-offs are rounded off to the nearest dime. The difference between the exact figure a horse should pay and the price it actually pays is called "Breakage". This breakage is shared equally between the State and the race track.

The totalisator board or the tote board, as it is commonly called, is a center of attraction. Most people going to the track spend more time acutally watching the tote board than they do watching the races. The tote board is part of the totalisator system that compiles and totals the money bet, thus determining the odds and pay-offs. As the tickets are sold, the information is electronically sent to the a control or tote room. Bets are continually totaled and the odds calculated, with the information automatically flashed on the tote board, which is usually prominently displayed in the infield. There is a lot of information posted on the tote board which includes; the odds of probable payoff, the track condition, the time of the race, the order of finish and pay-off of the race, the Win, Place, and Show pools, the total amount of money wagered in the

20

Trifecta, Perfecta, or Daily Double pools, the photo finish sign that lights up when appropriate, and the official sign that we talked about earlier, that declares the race official.

Many people watch the tote board to see if any drastic changes in the odds take place that might reflect a large amount of money bet on a particular horse. Others watch the board to watch for overlays. An overlay is when the chances of winning are greater than the odds indicate. A horse that in all probability figures to go off at 2 to 1 and is currently 4 to 1, is an overlay.

After you decide which horse to bet, how much money to bet, and how you want to place your bet, it's time to go to the windows. The betting windows at each track are not all the same. Some tracks have specific windows for each type of bet. At tracks with this type of system, there are windows for different denominations of Win tickets, Place tickets, and Show tickets. There are also separate windows for gimmick races. There are also special cashier windows where you cash your winning tickets.

The newer and more modern type of system is the All Betting and Cashing system. This system allows you to make any type of wager, Win, Place, Show, Daily Double, etc., bet any amount of money, on any race, and cash your ticket at any of the mutual windows. This type of system saves you a lot of time standing in line, and helps prevent you from getting shut out, which means not being able to place your bet before the start of the race.

When getting your tickets, tell the clerk the number of your horse as it is listed in the Program, not the name of the horse. Keep in mind also that the post position of the horse may not be the same in the newspapers as it is in the Program, due to other horses scratching out of the race. That is why it is necessary to always use the number listed in the

Program to bet your horse.

The Program number of the horse is usually the same as the post position, with the exception of races that have entries or fields. An Entry consists of two or more horses owned or trained by the same person racing as a unit in the betting. A bet on an entry will pay-off if either horse finishes in the position wagered. When horses are listed as number 1 and 1A, it denotes an entry. Just because the horse is listed as number 1 in the Program it does not mean that it will start the race from the number one post position. The post position generally will be listed just under the Program number.

Due to the fact that pari-mutuel machines can handle only twelve betting units in each race, it becomes necessary to establish a field if the race has over twelve entries. The extra horses are grouped together as a single betting unit. Because of the increased possibility of winning, only long shots are placed in the field. It is usually the responsibility of the Racing Secretary to select the horses that are to be placed in the field. The horses that the Racing Secretary selects are generally long shots or horses that he feels are least likely to win the race. What increases the possibility of winning, when betting the fields is, the fact that if any horse in the mutuel field wins the race and you are holding a winning ticket for the field, then you would win your bet.

If you are at a race track that has an All Betting System, you would first tell the clerk the number of the race, that is if it is different than the race they are currently taking bets on, then the amount of money you want to bet, and type of bet you want to make, either Win, Place, Show, Daily Double, etc., and then the program number of the horse.

Make sure you have your selections and your money ready when you get to the mutual window. Keep in mind that there will always be someone behind you waiting to try to get their bet in before the start of the race. If you spend an unnecessary amount of time at the window, someone behind you could get shut out.

If you have made your bet early, you may have time to go to the paddock and view the horses as they are saddled and prepared for the race. It is there that the jockeys receive last-minute instructions from the trainer as to how the horses are to be ridden in the race.

Ten minutes before post time, the announcement, "Riders Up", is sounded in the paddock, and the traditional bugle call of "Boots and Saddles" is sounded over the public address system, which signifies the start of the Post Parade. In the Post Parade the horses and riders are paraded in front of the grandstands. It gives the patrons a chance to view their horses in motion and yell their encouragement to the jockeys.

After the Post Parade, the horses are quickly warmed up and taken to the starting gates where they are loaded for the start of the race.

There is nothing more exciting than a horse race. The excitement of the crowd is something to behold as the horses charge out of the starting gate at the start of the race, and continue to maintain or better their position until the stretch finish, when the horse and jockey go all out to be the first to the finish line. If you are fortunate enough to have selected a horse in the lead, or charging for it, you will soon find the excitement of the race overwhelming you. There is nothing as exciting as a close race. especially if the horse you selected is victorious.

THE DAILY RACING FORM

The Daily Racing Form supplies the necessary material to properly handicap a race. Trying to handicap a race without a Racing Form is like trying to drive a car without wheels or tires.

In the Racing Form you will find all the information and material necessary to assist you in making a proper selection. The Racing Form contains past performances, jockey and trainer standings, latest workouts, result charts, selections, and a multitude of other information.

There are many ways to evaluate and consider available information. Some people use various systems, graphs, angles, tabulations, etc. Others use calculators and even computers. Whatever procedure a handicapper may use, the main thing to remember is the more information that is used and considered in making a decision, generally, the better the decision. This does not mean that it will be the right decision, because anything can happen in a horse race; but it definately will be a more educated decision.

24

From the past performances you will find the date of the horses most recent race, the number of the race and the track the race was at, the distance and fractional times of the race, the final time of the winner of the race, the track condition, the approximate closing odds, the weight carried in the race, the position of the horse at various points of the race, the position of the horse at the finish of the race and the number of lengths behind the winner, or if the winner, the number of lengths or distance the horse won by.

Also, listed will be the jockey and the post position they started from, the type of race, the speed rating, the first three finishers, along with the number of starters in the race. Just above the past performances you will find the color, sex, age, sire, dam, the dams sire, the owner, trainer, breeder, the state the horse was foaled in, and the lifetime earnings of the horse. The number of starts, the number of times the horse finished first, second, or third for the current and previous year are listed along with the turf course record.

Just below the past performances, you will find the latest workouts which will give you an indication of how good the horse has been working.

As you can see, there are many things to consider in selecting a horse. The Racing Form supplies the information, but you must evaluate it, and try to make the right decision.

EXPLANATION OF DAILY RACING FORM PAST PERFORMANCES

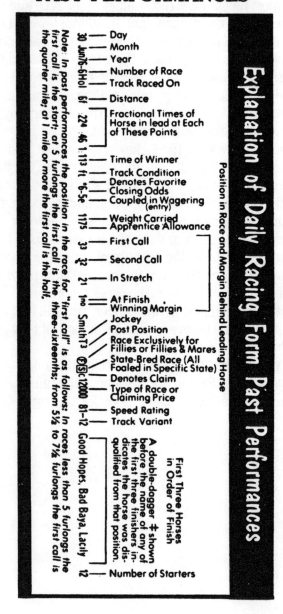

Explanation of Daily Racing Form Past Performances

- Day
- Month
- Year
- Number of Race
- Track Raced On
- Distance
- Fractional Times of Horse in lead at Each of These Points
- Time of Winner
- Track Condition
- Denotes Favorite
- Closing Odds
- Coupled in Wagering (entry)
- Weight Carried
- Apprentice Allowance
- First Call
- Second Call
- In Stretch
- At Finish
- Winning Margin
- Jockey
- Post Position
- Race Exclusively for Fillies or Fillies & Mares
- State-Bred Race (All Foaled in Specific State)
- Denotes Claim
- Type of Race or Claiming Price
- Speed Rating
- Track Variant
- Number of Starters

30 Jun76-6Hol 6f :22¾ :46 1:11³ ft *.6-5e 117⁵ 3³ 2² 2¹ 1ⁿᵒ SmithT³ ⒻⓈⒸlc12000 81-12 Good Hopes, Bad Baya, Lacily 12

Position in Race and Margin Behind Leading Horse

First Three Horses in Order of Finish

A double-dagger ‡ shown before the name of any of the first three finishers indicates the horse was disqualified from that position.

Note: In past performances the position in the race for "first call" is as follows: In races less than 5 furlongs the first call is the start; at 5 furlongs the first call is the three-sixteenths; from 5½ to 7½ furlongs the first call is the quarter mile; at 1 mile or more the first call is the half.

26

PAST PERFORMANCE POINTERS

ABBREVIATIONS USED IN POINTS OF CALL

no-nose   hd-head   nk-neck

WORKOUTS

Each horse's most recent workouts appear under the past performances. For example, Jly 20 Hol 3f :38b indicates the horse worked on July 20 at Hollywood Park. The distance of the work was 3 furlongs over a fast track and the horse was timed in 38 seconds, breezing. A "bullet" ● appearing before the date of a workout indicates that the workout was the best of the day for that distance at that track.

The Bullet ● Symbol Hits the Spot In
Past Performance Workout Lines

● Jun 25 Hol 4f ft :46h

The bullet indicates the workout was the best of the day at
the track for the distance. The ● makes it easy to spot.

ABBREVIATIONS USED IN WORKOUTS:
b—breezing   d—driving   e—easily   g—worked from gate
h—handily   bo—bore out   tc—turf course   Tr—trial race
trt following track abbreviation indicates
horse worked on training track

RACES RANKED in ORDER OF IMPORTANCE
Races in the order of their relative importance are grouped
roughly as follows, stakes events, of course, being tops:

Stakes (allowance, handicap, weight-for-age, scale weight.)

Overnight races (allowance, weight-for-age, special
weights, handicaps.)

Graded allowance races and graded handicaps.

Maiden and maiden allowance races.

Combination races.

Claiming races.

The importance of a match race is dependent upon the
quality or popularity of the contestants. It might overshadow
a stake event, or engage mere platers.

The importance of a claiming handicap or stake, also is
dependent upon the quality of the horses, as indicated by their
entered price.

RECORD OF STARTS AND EARNINGS

The horse's racing record for his most recent two years of competition appears to the extreme right of the name of the breeder and is referred to as his "money lines". This lists the year, number of starts, wins, seconds, thirds and earnings. The letter "M" is in the lower line only, it indicates the horse was a maiden at the end of that year.

TURF COURSE RECORD

The horse's turf course record shows his lifetime starts, wins, seconds, thirds and earnings on the grass and appears directly below his money lines.

LIFETIME RECORD

The horse's lifetime record shows his career races, wins, seconds, thirds, and total earnings. The statistics, updated with each start, include all his races—on dirt, grass and over jumps—and is located under the trainer's name.

DISTANCE

a—preceding distance (a6f) denotes "about" distance (about 6 furlongs in this instance).

FOREIGN TRACKS

♦ —before track abbreviation indicates it is located in a foreign country.

29

RACES OTHER THAN ON MAIN DIRT TRACK

•̲ —following distance denotes inner dirt course.
Ⓣ —following distance indicates turf (grass) course race.
T̲ —following distance indicates inner turf course.
[S]—following distance indicates steeplechase race.
[H]—following distance indicates hurdle race.

TRACK CONDITIONS

ft—fast   fr—frozen   gd—good   sl—slow   sy—sloppy
m—muddy   hy—heavy
Turf courses, including steeplechase and hurdles:
hd—hard   fm—firm   gd—good   yl—yielding   sf—soft

SYMBOLS ACCOMPANYING CLOSING ODDS

* (preceding)—favorite   e (following)—entry
f (following)—mutuel field

APPRENTICE OR RIDER WEIGHT ALLOWANCES

Allowance indicated by superior figure following
weight—117^5.

TODAY'S WEIGHT

With the exception of assigned-weight handicap races, weights are computed according to the conditions of the race. Weight includes the rider and his equipment, saddle, lead pads, etc., and takes into account the apprentice allowance of pounds claimed. It does not include a jockey's overweight, which is announced by track officials prior to the race. The number of pounds claimed as on apprentice allowance is shown by a superior (small) figure to the right of the weight—117.

RACE CLASSIFICATION

10000—Claiming race (eligible to be claimed for $10,000). Note: The letter c preceding claiming price (c 10000) indicates horse was claimed.

M10000—Maiden claiming race (non-winners—eligible to be claimed).

10000H—Claiming handicap (eligible to be claimed).

^{0}10000—Optional claiming race (entered NOT to be claimed).

10000^0—Optional claiming race (eligible to be claimed).

Mdn—Maiden race (non-winners).

AlwM—Maiden allowance race (for non-winners with special weight allowances).

Aw10000—Allowance race with purse value.

HcpO—Overnight handicap race.

SplW—Special weight race.

Wfa—Weight-for-age race.

Mtch—Match race.

A10000—Starter allowance race (horses who have started for claiming price shown, or less, as stipulated in the conditions).

H10000—Starter handicap (same restriction as above).

S10000—Starter special weight (restricted as above). Note: Where no amount is specified in conditions of "starters" race, dashes are substituted as shown below:

$$A\text{\_\_\_\_}\qquad H\text{\_\_\_\_}\qquad S\text{\_\_\_\_}$$

50000S—Claiming stakes (eligible to be claimed).

31

STAKES RACES

In stakes races, with the exception of claiming stakes, the name or abbreviation of name is shown in the class of race column. The letter "H" after the name indicates the race was a handicap stakes. The same procedure is used for the rich invitational races for which there are no nomination or starting fees. The letters "Inv" following the abbrevitaion indicate the race was by invitation only.

SPEED RATINGS

This is a comparison of the horse's final time with the track record established prior to the opening of the racing season at that track. The track record is given a rating of 100. One point is deducted for each fifth of a second by which a horse fails to equal the track record (one length is approximately equal to one-fifth of a second). Thus, in a race in which the winner equals the track record (a Speed Rating of 100), another horse who is beaten 12 lengths (or an estimated two and two-fifths seconds) receives a Speed Rating of 88 (100 minus 12). If a horse breaks the track record he receives an additional point for each one-fifth second by which he lowers the record (if the track record is 1:10 and he is timed in 1:09 3/5, his Speed Rating is 102). In computing beaten-off distances for Speed Ratings, fractions of one-half length or more are figured as one full length (one point). No Speed Ratings are given for steeplechase or hurdle events, for races of less than three furlongs, or for races for which the horse's speed rating is less than 25.

When Daily Racing Form prints its own time, in addition to the official track time, the Speed Rating is based on the official track time.

Note: Speed Ratings for new distances are computed and

assigned when adequate time standards are established.

TODAY'S CLAIMING PRICE
If a horse is entered to be claimed, the price for which he may be claimed appears in bold face type to the right of the trainer's name.

FOREIGN-BRED HORSES
An asterisk (*) preceding the name of the horse
indicates foreign-bred.
(No notation is made for horses bred in Canada and Cuba)

MUD MARKS
✳–Fair mud runner   X—Good mud runner
Ⓧ —Superior mud runner

SEX
c—colt h—horse g—gelding rig—ridgling f—filly m—mare

PEDIGREE
Each horse's pedigree lists, in the order named, color, sex, age, sire, dam, and grandsire (sire of dam).

BREEDER

Abbreviation following breeder's name indicates the state, Canadian province, place of origin or foreign country in which the horse was foaled.

EXPLANATION OF TRACK VARIANT

This takes into consideration all of the races run on a particular day and could reflect either the quality of the competition, how many points below par the track happened to be or both. The speed rating of each winner is added together, then an average is taken based on the number of races run. This average is deducted from the track par of 100 and the difference is the track variant (example: average speed ratings of winners involved is 86; par is 100; the Track Variant is 14). When there is a change in the track condition during the course of a program the following procedure is employed in compiling the variant: Races run on dirt tracks classified as fast, frozen or good, and those listed as hard, firm or good on the turf, are used in striking one average. Strips classified as slow, sloppy, muddy or heavy on the dirt, or yielding and soft on the turf, are grouped for another average.

If all the races on a program are run in either one or the other of these general classifications only one average is used. The lower the variant the faster the track or the better overall the quality of competition.

TROUBLE LINES

When a horse experiences trouble in a race, this information is reported, with the date of the incident, in a capsule description directly below the past performance line for that race.

34

DEAD-HEATS, DISQUALIFICATIONS

◖ following the finish call indicates this horse was part of a dead-heat (an explanatory line appears under that past performance line).

† following the finish call indicates this horse was disqualified. The official placing appears under the past performance line. An explanatory line also appears under the past performances of each horse whose official position was changed due to the disqualificaion.

‡ before the name of any of the first three finishers indicates the horse was disqualified from that position.

POST POSITION

Horse's post position appears after jockey's name—Smith T³.

FILLY OR FILLY-MARE RACES

Ⓕ —preceding the race classification indicates races exclusively for fillies or fillies and mares.

RESTRICTED RACES

⑤ —preceding the race classification denotes state-bred races restricted to horses bred in a certain state (or a given geographic area) which qualify under state breeding programs.

Ⓡ —preceding the race classifiction indicates races that have certain eligibility restrictions other than sex or age.

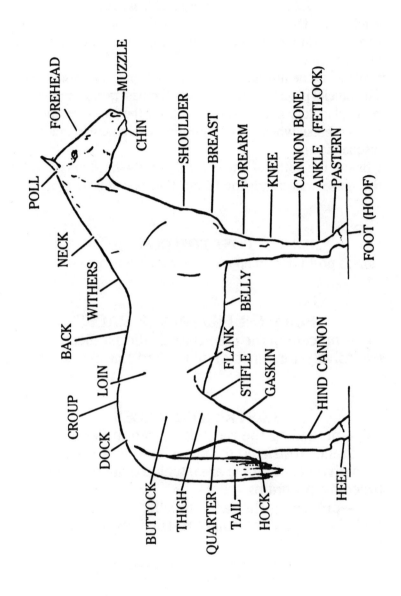

POLL
FOREHEAD
MUZZLE
CHIN
NECK
SHOULDER
BREAST
FOREARM
KNEE
CANNON BONE
ANKLE (FETLOCK)
PASTERN
FOOT (HOOF)
WITHERS
BACK
LOIN
CROUP
DOCK
BUTTOCK
THIGH
QUARTER
TAIL
HOCK
FLANK
STIFLE
GASKIN
BELLY
HIND CANNON
HEEL

NAMING A THOROUGHBRED

Naming a Thoroughbred is not the simple process as it might seem. Names submitted by owners must conform to the rules and regulations set forth by The Jockey Club and must be approved by their Stewards. Names are limited to 18 letters (spaces and punctuation marks count as letters) with no limitation on the number of words.

Names that have been used during the previous 15 years, either in the stud or in racing, cannot be duplicated and names cannot be claimed for unregistered horses, although those which are eligible may be reserved for one year. Names of stallions whose daughters are in stud, names of famous or notorious persons and trade names or names of commerical significance are not acceptable. Names which bear any suggestive, vulgar or obscene meaning are prohibited.

Identical prefixes or suffixes may not be used by any owner in naming horses bred or owned by him. The usage of 2nd, 3rd, etc., even though spelled out, may not be used in names.

Names of famous horses and names whose spelling or pronunciation are similar to those already used are restricted. Copyrighted names (titles of books, songs, movies, etc.) may be used five years after those names were first introduced. Names of living persons are allowed only if written permission is filed with The Jockey Club, individually, by the person whose names are to be used. When foreign words or names are requested, an English translation must be furnished. "Coined"
or "made-up" names must be accompanied with an explanation. An owner may change the name of a horse prior to January 1 of the 2-year-old year. After that date permission must be granted by the Stewards of The Jockey Club. However, no change will be permitted after a horse has started.

Owners usually submit additional names as alternates in case their first choice is not approved. Some owners combine a part of the sire's name with that of the mare's in naming thoroughbreds. The late Col. E.R. Bradley gave his horses names beginning with the letter "B". Brookfield Farm has used "I" as the first letter in naming its thoroughbreds.

(Reprinted from American Racing Manual)

COLOR ABBREVIATIONS

"b" bay (varies from a light yellowish tan [light bay] to a dark, rich shade, almost brown, and between these, a bright mahogany [blood bay]. A bay always has black mane and tail).

"br" brown (sometimes difficult to tell from black or dark bay, but can be distinguished by noting the fine tan or brown hairs on the muzzle or flanks).

"blk" black (if any doubt arises in distinguishing between dark brown and black, the black can be determined by noting the fine black hairs on the muzzle).

"ch" chestnut (varies from a dark liver color to a light, washy yellow, between which comes the brilliant red gold and copper shades. A chestnut never has black mane, tail or points.).

"dk b or br" describes horses whose color is marginal, as well as those which are brown.

"gr" gray (mixture of white hairs and black, sometimes scarcely distinguishable from black at birth, getting lighter with age).

"ro" roan (there are two classes—red or strawberry, produced by intermingling of black, white and yellow hairs).

"wh" white (predominantly white coloring—very rare).
NOTE: Effective with the registration of foals of 1963, individual designations as "dark bay" and "brown" have been dropped, and term "dark bay or brown" has been adopted.

MARKINGS OF A THOROUGHBRED

HEAD MARKINGS

STAR—A collection of white hair found on the forehead.

STRIPE—A white marking starting at the eye level or below and extending to or above the upper lip.

SNIP—A separate white or flesh colored marking found between the nostrils or on the lips.

BALD—A white face which includes the eyes, nostrils and upper lip.

LEG MARKINGS

WHITE CORONET—A small area, circling the leg immediately above the hoof, which is white.

SPOTS ON THE CORONET—Dark spots on a white coronet.

HALF WHITE PASTERN—The lower half of the pastern is white.

THREE-QUARTERS WHITE PASTERN—The lower three-quarters of the pastern is white.

WHITE PASTERN—The entire pastern is white.

WHITE PASTERN AND PART OF ANKLE—The white marking extends up to and includes part of the ankle.

FULL WHITE ANKLE—The white marking extends up to and includes the entire ankle.

QUARTER WHITE STOCKING—The white marking extends up to and includes the lower one-quarter of the cannon.

HALF WHITE STOCKING—The white marking extends up to and includes the lower half of the cannon.

THOROUGHBRED RACING TERMS

ACEY-DEUCY   When the jockey has his right stirrup shorter then the left so that he can easily equalize his weight on the turns.

ACROSS THE BOARD   To bet an equal amount of money to win, place, and show.

ADDED MONEY   Money added by the racing association to amount paid by owners through nominations, eligibilty, and starting fees.

AGAINST THE BOYS   A term used in referring to a filly or mare competing against colts, geldings, or stallions.

AGE   The classification of a horse that approximates the age of a horse. The universal birthday for all horses is January 1st. A horse foaled in May will be classified as a yearling on the following January. Likewise a horse foaled in December will be one year old a month later. This is the reason that breeders breed their mares for an early foalings.

AGED HORSE   A horse four years old or older.

AGENT   There are three types of agents; owner's authorized agent, trainer's authorized agent, and jockey agents. Each is authorized to represent their appointee's for different duties.

AIRING	A horse that is winning, but not running at it's best.
ALL BETTING SYSTEM	A system that allows you to make any type of wager, win, place, show, daily double, etc., bet any amount of money, on any race, and cash your ticket, at any of the mutual windows.
ALL OUT	When a horse is being ridden at its highest speed, doing it's very best, in a race or workout.
ALLOWANCE RACE	The Racing Secretary assigns conditions, and weights according to a horses' past preformance record, and present condition, in order that horses of similar caliber will be in competition.
ALLOWANCES	Weights and other conditions of a race.
ALLOWANCE STAKES RACE	An allowance race that is raced under the usual stakes conditions, such as subscriptions, entrance and starting fees.
A LOCK	A sure winner.
ALSO ELIGIBLE	A horse officially entered in a race but not allowed to start unless other scratches are incurred.
ALSO RAN	A horse that finished out of the money.
ALTER	To castrate a horse, also called cut.

45

AMERICAN RACING MANUAL	An annual publication compiled and published by the Daily Racing Form. It deals with the racing events of the previous year and the history of the sport, in this country and others.
AMERICAN STUD BOOK	The record book of all North American Thoroughbreds.
ANGLES	Significant information sometimes overlooked by handicappers concerned with basic factors.
ANKLE	That part of the leg of a horse between the cannon and pastern. Also called Fetlock.
ANKLE BOOT	A protective covering that is placed over the fetlock.
ANKLE CUTTER	A horse that injures the inside of its fetlock joint while racing or exercising.
APPEAL	A request for a Board of Review to investigate and review an official ruling.
APPRENTICE	A beginning jockey who has not won forty races or completed three years of riding, since his fifth victory.
APPRENTICE ALLOWANCE	A weight concession granted to an apprentice jockey.

APPRENTICE CONTRACT

A contract between an apprentice jockey and an owner or trainer. The terms of these contracts vary, but are often prescribed by the Racing Commission.

ARM

The limb or bone of a horse between the shoulder and the elbow.

A SHOT

A chance to win.

ASSISTANT STARTER

Employees of the race track whose duty it is to help load the horses into the starting gate and help to hold unruly horses until the start of the race.

ASSISTANT TRAINER

An employee whose duty it is to help the trainer, and perform duties specified by him in connection with the training and caring for horses in his care. Some Racing Commissions license assistant trainers as such, and others issue a regular trainers license to them.

AT HOME IN THE GOING

A term used to describe a horse that is racing it's best with the conditions of the racing surface, such as a sloppy track, etc. A horse that seems to be comfortable with the track condition.

AT STUD

A stallion that is used for breeding purposes, to sire foals.

AT THE POST	When the horses reach the starting gate in a race, but are not yet in the gate.
AUTOMATIC BET OR PLAY	When a horse is fit and seems to have a definite advantage over its competitors, is an automatic bet or play.
AWAY	Starting the race; the horses got away from the gate.
BABY	A two year old horse.
BABY RACE	A race for two year olds.
BACKSIDE	The stable area.
BACKSIDE OF TRACK	Same as backstretch: the straightaway part of the track on the far side, between turns.
BACKSTRETCH	The straightaway part of the track on the far side, between turns.
BAD ACTOR	An unwilling or tough horse.
BAD DOER	A horse with a poor appetite.
BADGE HORSE	A horse that is poor or crippled that is used for the purpose of acquiring an owner's license in order to receive the benefits, such as free admission to the track, etc.

BADGE LIST   Trainers list which includes all his owners and employees.

BAD LEGGED   A horse with an injured or sore leg or legs. It usually refers to a horse with chronic leg problems.

BAD STARTER   A horse that is difficult to handle at the start of a race, either due to being tempermental, nervous or unfamiliar with the starting gates.

BALD   A horse having a white face including the eyes and nostrils, or parts thereof.

BALKING   When a horse stops or shys at an obstacle, and refuses to act or continue.

BALL   Medicine administered to a horse orally. Commonly a physic.

BALLING GUN   A device used to administer pills to a horse.

BANDAGE   Strips of cloth wound around the lower part of a horses' leg for support or protection against injury.

BANGTAIL   A horses' tail cut horizontally across. A slang term used for a race horse.

BAR PLATE	A horseshoe with a bar across the heel that is usually used for the protection of quarter cracks or other corrective measures.
BARN SOUR	A horse that continually tries to return to the barn area, is said to be barn sour.
BARREL	The round part of a horses body, between the forequarters and the hindquarters.
BARREN	A mare that is not in foal after being bred.
BARRIER	Starting gate or device used to start a race.
BAT	A jockey's whip or crop.
BATTERY	An illegal device used to prod a horse, by shocking it, to make it run faster.
BAY	A color of a horse which varies from a light yellowish tan to a dark shade almost brown, and also include bright mahogany. Bays have black manes and tails and black points.
BEARING (IN or OUT)	A horse going to one side or the other, not in a straight line.

BELL	Signal sounding the opening of the starting gate, and the closing off of pari-mutuel wagering.
BELMONT STAKES	A 1½ mile stakes race for 3 year old racehorses that is held annually at Belmont Park in New York. It is the third race of the Thoroughbred Triple Crown.
BEND	The end or turn of an eliptical race track.
BEST BET	The selection of a handicapper which he feels is the horse most likely to win it's race on a given day.
BEST TIME	The fastest time a horse has raced a specified distance.
BET	A wager. Money risked or staked on an uncertain event, namely a horse race.
BETTING COUP	When a trainer conspires to set up a race for his horse that makes his horse go off at big odds.
BETTING POOL	The amount of money bet on each horse in the race, which determines the odds on the horses in the race.
BIB	A device that attaches under a horses mouth to prevent it from chewing.

BIG 6	A wager where you must select the winner of six successive races. Same as Sweep Six.
BIG RACE	A horse that runs a big race is a horse that raced extremely well in tough company, regardless of whether it won or lost the race.
BILL DALY	When a jockey breaks his horse in front and sets the pace, he is said to be "On the Bill Daly", named after a colorful trainer who raced prior to the turn of the century, who instilled this manner of riding into his jockeys.
BIT	A device used in a horse's mouth to guide or control it.
BLACK LETTERS	The fastest workout at a certain distance for the day; also called a bullet workout.
BLACKSMITH	A person that puts shoes on a horse, also called a farrier or platter.
BLACK TYPE	Denotes a Stakes Winner or a Stakes Placed Horse. To receive Black Type, a horse must finish first, second, or third in an added money race in which entries close 72 hours before the race, has an entry fee paid by the owner, and an added purse value of at least $15,000. In a Grade 1 Stake Race, the first four finishers receive Black Type.

BLANKET FINISH	When a group of horses finish a race so closely as to be able to put a blanket on them.
BLAZE	A blaze is a large patch of white hair that runs down the face of a horse.
BLEEDER	A horse that hemorrhages from the respiratory tract during or after a race or workout.
BLEEDERS LIST	A list of all bleeders which is maintained by the track veterinarian.
BLEMISH	A scar that is left from an injury or wound.
BLIND BLINKERS	A set of blinkers that has one full cup that completely blinds a horses' one eye. This type of blinker is sometimes used on a horse that is blind in one eye to prevent dirt from being thrown in that eye.
BLIND SWITCH	When a horse is caught in a pocket or between horses where he cannot pursue a desired course.
BLINKERS	A device used to limit a horses vision.
BLISTER	An ointment or liquid used as a counter irritant to promote healing.

BLOCK HEEL   A type of racing shoe with raised blocks to prevent a horse from running down.

BLOODLINES   The heritage of a horse.

BLOOD HORSE (THE)   A weekly publication published by the Thoroughbred Owners and Breeders Association.

BLOOD HORSE   A term that refers to a Thoroughbred Race Horse.

BLOODSTOCK   A term used in referring to Thoroughbred horses used in either racing or breeding.

BLOODWORMS   A parasite that gets into the bloodstream of a horse.

BLOW A STIRRUP   A term used when a jockey looses a stirrup, or his foot comes out of the stirrup, during a race or work-out.

BLOW OUT   A workout usually before the day of the race.

BLOW UP   A term used to describe swelling in a horse's leg usually due to an injury.

BLOW THE TURN   A horse that ran wide in the turn.

BLUE GRASS COUNTRY	An area in Kentucky centered around Lexington. It is an area in which the grass has a blueish-green color. This area is rich in lime and phosphates and is considered to be ideal for the breeding and raising of horses.
BOARD	Same as the tote board; a sign that displays information on the race.
BOAT RACE	A term used in referring to a fixed race.
BODY BRUSH	A short bristled brush that is used to remove dust and dirt from a horse's coat.
BOLT	Suddenly veering from a straight course.
BOLTER	A horse that has a habit of bolting in a race.
BOOK	A person who accepts bets, also called a bookmaker.
BOOK	Refers to the Condition Book which is drafted by the Racing Secretary and tells the types of races available, along with the different requirements for each race.
BOOK (Jockey's)	A list of horses that a jockey is committed to ride, taken from a condition book, usually handled by a jockey agent.

BOOK RACE	A race that is taken from the Condition Book.
BOOKIE	A slang term referring to a bookmaker.
BOOKMAKER	A person who accepts bets.
BOOT HOME	To win a race by the jockey using his heels or spurs to urge a horse to run its best.
BOOTS AND SADDLES	The traditional bugle call that is sounded to signify the starting of the post parade.
BOOT TICKETS	A win ticket that is bought for a jockey by an owner or trainer and given to the jockey or placed in his boot, while in the paddock, before the start of the race, to try to induce the jockey to put an extra effort into winning the race.
BOTTOM	The stamina in a horse. Also the sub-surface of a racing strip.
BOTTOM LINE	Breeding on the female or distaff side.
BOTTOM SIDE	A horses' breeding ancestry on the dam's side; also called the bottom line.
BOWED	A word used in place of or referring to a bowed tendon.

BOWED TENDON — Also called Tendonitis or bowed. A rupture or partial rupture of the sheath that encloses the flexor tendon, which usually results from a severe strain of one or both flexor tendons.

BOX (The) — Refers to the steam room that the jockeys use to sweat off unwanted pounds.

BOX (Betting) — To bet all possible combinations of three or more horses.

BOXED IN — When a horse is in a pocket in a race, with a horse in front, and along side it.

BOY — Another name for a jockey.

BRACE — A rubdown liniment used on a horse after a race or workout.

BRACE BANDAGE — A bandage used to support and protect a horse from skinning its legs, while racing. They are also used on a horse in a stall or while a horse is being shipped in a van.

BRAN — A grain that is ground and usually dampened, that aids a horse in digestion and acts as a mild laxative.

BREAK — To take off or start from the starting gates.

57

BREAK	To train a young horse to carry a rider and respond to his actions.
BREAKAGE	The difference between the exact figure a horse should pay and the price paid. A horse that should pay $56.28 would only pay $56.20. The .08 difference would be the breakage.
BREAK DOWN	When a horse suffers an injury or lameness.
BREAK IN	A horse who at the start of a race veers toward the inner rail.
BREAKS IN THE AIR	It's when a horse is standing on its hind legs when the starting gates open and leaps up, instead of ahead, at the start of a race.
BREAK MAIDEN	When a horse or jockey wins the first race of their career.
BREAK ON TOP	To get out of the starting gates first.
BREAK OUT	A horse who at the start of a race veers towards the outer rail.
BREATHER	Holding back the horse for a short distance in a race to conserve his speed or strength; letting the horse catch its breath.

BREAST COLLAR	A strap that goes around a horse's chest to prevent the saddle from slipping.
BRED	A horse is considered bred at the place of its birth. If a foal is born in Illinois, then it is an Illinois Bred Foal.
BRED BY	Used in this manner it denotes the sire of a particular horse.
BREEDER	In the Thoroughbred Breeders Program the Breeder is the owner of the mare at the time of foaling.
BREEDERS CUP SERIES	Breeders Cup Series is a multi-million dollar program designed to create new fan interest in Thoroughbred racing and to provide the industry with a far-reaching and effective promotional tool. The program is funded by nominations of stallions and the nominations of those stallions offerings. The Beeders Cup event day will consist of races with a combined total of $10 million in purses. Another 12 million in supplementary awards will be distributed in stakes supplemented races, at race tracks throughout the U.S. and Canada.
BREEDING	The mating of horses.
BREEZE	To work a horse at a brisk pace as you would in a race.

BREEZING A pace that is referred to in a race or workout describing an easy pace, slower than handily but faster than easily.

BRIDLE The headgear for a horse that is used to control and steer it.

BRITTLE FEET A problem in which the horney part of a horse's hoof becomes dry and brittle.

BROKE DOWN A horse that has suffered an injury or has pulled up lame and cannot be raced for a considerable time.

BROKEN DOWN HORSE PLAYER A term used by Dave Feldman, a Chicago horseman and newspaper columnist, describing a person who frequents the race track and places bets on a regular basis.

BROKEN WIND The breakdown of the air vesicles of a horse's lungs, caused by strain or excessive feeding before a strenuous exercise.

BROODMARE A female horse used for breeding.

BROODMARE DAM A dam whose daughters have distinguished themselves as producers.

BROODMARE SIRE A sire whose daughters have distinguished themselves as producers.

BRUSH To groom or clean a horse.

BRUSHING   An injury to the fetlock caused by a strike from the opposite foot.

BUG   An apprentice weight allowance.

BUG BOY   An apprentice jockey.

BULLET   The bullet • indicates that the workout was the best of the day at the track for the distance. The • makes it easy to spot. Denotes a black letter work.

BULL RING   A small race track. Usually refers to a five-eighths mile track.

BUMP   When a horse is sideswiped or run into by another horse in a race.

BUM STEER   Wrong information.

BUSH TRACK   A minor race track.

BUTE   Butazolidine, a pain killing medication.

BUY THE RACK   To buy all possible combinations of daily double or quinella tickets to insure receiving the winning bet. A bettor may take a pick in one race and buy the rack or all the combinations in the second race to insure that if his horse wins that he also wins the Daily Double.

BY	A word denoting the sire of a horse. A horse that is by Native Dancer means that Native Dancer was the sire or father of that horse.
BUZZER	An illegal device used to prod a horse by shocking it.
CALF-KNEED	A horse whose forelegs bend backwards at the knees.
CALK	A piece on the bottom of the shoe to give a horse a better grip.
CALL	A fast and incomplete description of the race. It is usually the mentioning of the leaders at any particular part of the track, thus comes the saying that a slow horse never got a call.
CALLER	The person who calls the running positions of the horses in a race.
CALL ON	When a jockey asks a horse to extend itself or to urge it to run faster by whatever means is necessary for the horse to respond, whipping, etc.
CAME FROM OUT OF IT	A horse that charged toward the lead, from behind a majority of the horses.

CAMERA
PATROL   Same as Film Patrol. A system whereby movies are taken from various locations around the track from different angles to insure that no infractions of rules happen during the race. These movies can be viewed by the Stewards within minutes after the finish of the race in the case of an inquiry.

CAMPAIGN   To operate a racing stable and compete with other trainers at a race track. Also a horse that competes.

CAMPAIGNER   A horse or trainer that goes from track to track as the seasons change throughout the year. Also a reliable horse.

CANNON   The part of a horses' foreleg between the knee and the ankle, on the hind leg, it is between the hock and the ankle.

CANNON BONE The bone in a horse's leg between the knee and the fetlock.

CANTER   A slow gallop.

CANTLE   The back part of a saddle.

CAPPED ELBOW A swelling of the elbow of a horse caused by injury.

CAPPED HOCK A swelling of the hock due to an injury.

63

CARD	The entire racing program scheduled for a particular day. A jockey that rode the card, rode a horse in every race that particular day.
CASH A TICKET	To win a bet or wager.
CASHIER	The person whose job it is to cash winning pari-mutuel tickets.
CAST	A horse caught in a position in a stall that he cannot get up.
CASTRATED	A male horse that has his testicles removed.
CENTER FIELD	The infield of a race track.
CHARITY DAY	A day of racing in which all or part of the proceeds are given to charity.
CHALK HORSE	The horse that is favored to win his race.
CHALK PLAYER	A player who usually bets the favorites in a race.
CHALLENGE	A horse that is close in on the leader or leaders in a race.
CHANGE LEADS	When a horse changes from leading with the left foot to leading with the right foot or vice-versa.

CHART BOOK   A compilation of racing charts in book form.

CHART   The number assigned to each race
NUMBER   run at all recognized race tracks on the North American Continent by a publication such as the Daily Racing Form.

CHARTS   The past performance charts of a horse as in the Racing Form.

CHECK   To suddenly alter or slow down the speed of a horse in a race.

CHESTNUT   A color of a horse that varies from dark liver color to a light washy yellow, between which come the brilliant red and copper shades. A chestnut horse never has a black mane or tail or other points. A chestnut is also a growth on the inside of every leg of a horse.

CHOPPY   It is the stride of a horse. It is a short awkward stride. Usually a horse refuses to stride out due to soreness or lameness. Although it is sometimes a natural characteristic, a horse that is choppy is usually sore.

CHUTE   A straight prolongation of any part of the racing strip from which a race can be started. Because races vary widely in their distances, a chute prevents a race from being started on a bend or curve of the track.

CIRCUIT   A number of race tracks in a given area that cooperate by agreeing on racing dates so that horsemen are inconvenienced as little as possible in shipping their horses from one track to another as the season progresses. Usually their dates do not overlap.

CLAIM   To make a written financial commitment to purchase a specific horse entered in a claiming race, for the claiming price specified, before the start of the race.

CLAIMER   A horse that is entered in or normally runs in a claiming race.

CLAIMING BOX   A compartment in which claims are placed.

CLAIMING PRICE   The predetermined price at which a horse in entered in a claiming race.

CLAIMING RACE   A horse entered in this type of race may be claimed for a specific amount by any registered owner of horses racing at the meeting in which the claiming race is held.

CLASS	A quality which separates superior blood lines, stamina, courage, endurance, ability and other ingredients necessary to make a winner.
CLERK OF THE SCALE	The official who weighs the jockeys before and after a race to insure that the proper weight is carried, and also carries out various other duties pertaining to the jockeys and jockey rooms.
CLIPPED HEELS	When the horse in the rear strikes the heels of the horse in front of him.
CLIMB	A horse that is having trouble getting a foothold, usually at the start of the race.
CLOCK	The stopwatch used to time a race or workout.
CLOCK IN YOUR HEAD	The ability of a jockey to be able to time a horse and to realize how fast he is going in order to conserve enough energy for a final run at the end of a race.
CLOCKER	The official who keeps the official time of the race and of all workouts.
CLOSE	To decrease the distance between a horse in a race and the leaders of the race; to come from behind.

CLOSED AT	The odds on the tote board at the start of the race. The last flash on the board, which is the price that determines the price a winning ticket pays.
CLOSED CLAIMING RACE	A claiming race in which the only owners eligible to claim a horse are the owners that have a horse entered in the race.
CLOSED FAST	A horse that finished fast.
CLOSED RACE	A race that imposes certain restrictions or conditions which can exclude certain horses.
CLOSER	A horse that comes from behind and closes the distance at the finish of the race.
CLOSING BELL	The bell that rings as the horses leave the starting gates, to indicate the closing off of pari-mutuel wagering.
CLOSING ODDS	The odds at the time the betting stops, just before the start of the race.
CLOSING STRIDES	The last few strides of a race.
CLUB HOUSE	A section of the racetrack pavilion reserved for special ticket holders, usually providing the choicest seats and other facilities such as a restaurant and bar.

CLUB HOUSE TURN	The turn or bend of track, at the point where the Club House is usually found, usually the first turn past the finish line.
COFFIN BONE	The principal or main bone in the horses foot.
COGGINS TEST	Gel Immuno-Diffusion method of testing a horse for equine infectious anemia. This method was developed by Dr. Leroy Coggins. A horse must be tested and present a negative "Coggins Test Certificate" before it is allowed entrance to any race track.
COLD WATER BANDAGES	Bandages that have been soaked in cold water before being applied to a horse.
COLIC	A term used to describe pain in the abdomen of the horse.
COLOR	The pigmentation of a horse, The Official colors of Thoroughbreds registered with the Jockey Club are: Bay, Brown, Chestnut, Black, Grey and Roan. The colors of Bay, Brown and Chestnut comprise approximately 90% of all horses registered.
COLOR ROOM	The room that is used to store and maintain the colors or silks, for the various owners, so they are readily available to the jockeys for racing.

COLORS	The racing silks worn by the jockey, denoting ownership of the horse.
COLT	A male horse from his second birthday until it reaches age five, at which time he is called a horse.
COMB	A metal toothed device used for arranging a horses mane or tail.
COMBINATION TICKET	A pari-mutuel ticket that shows an equal amount of money bet to WIN, PLACE, and SHOW. One $6.00 ticket is equal to one $2.00 WIN, one $2.00 PLACE, and one $2.00 SHOW ticket.
COMBO	Same as combination.
COME FROM BEHIND	It is when a horse comes from behind the rest of the horses, towards the end of the race, to challenge for the lead.
COMES FROM OUT OF IT	It is when a horse races from behind the rest of the horses, towards the end of the race, to challenge for the lead.
CONDITION	To get a horse ready to race.
CONDITION BOOK	A book made by the Racing Secretary that tells the types of races available, along with the different requirements for each race.

CONDITIONS	The requirements set down for a particular race; maidens, nonwinners of two races, etc. It also includes distance and type of race.
CONFORMATION	The physical structure of a horse.
CONSENSUS	The opinion of the majority of unofficial handicappers as to the order in which horses in a race will finish and which horse will Win, usually this is done in a publication such as the Racing Form who has more than one handicapper.
CONSOLATION DOUBLE	When a person is holding a Daily Double ticket that includes the winner of the first race and a horse that is scratched from the second race, the holder receives a proportion of the money bet on the pool.
CONTINGENCY	The sale of a horse where all or part of the purchase price is payable out of winning purses of the horse, for its new owners.
CONTRACT	A written agreement between a stable owner and a jockey whereby the jockey agrees to ride first call and, or, other conditions as set forth in the agreement.
CONTRACT RIDER	A jockey under contract to a certain stable.

71

COOLER	A light blanket or sheet placed over a horse after a race, or workout, while he is being hot walked.
COOLING OUT	To walk a horse to his normal condition after he becomes overheated in a workout or race.
CORDED UP	The muscles across the back of a horse over the kidneys become tense or taut, this usually happens when a horse is raced and not in condition. If a horse is corded up after a workout it tells the trainer that the horse is not yet ready to race.
CORONARY BAND	The tissue around the top of a horses hoof.
CORONET	The part of a horses leg just above the hoof.
CORRAL	A pen or enclosure for horses, that allows a horse to get more exercise than it normally would confined in a stall.
CORRECTED WEIGHTS	When the weight assigned a horse is changed, after the entries have been released by the Racing Secretary.
COUPLED	Two or more horses running, as an entry, and a single betting unit in a race.
COURSE	A term used to describe the racing strip.

COVER A term used to describe a stallion breeding a mare; the act of copulation.

COW HOCKS When a horses hocks are turned inwards like a cow.

COW KICK When a horse kicks forward and to one side, with it's hind leg.

CRADLE A device that attaches onto a horse's neck to prevent it from lowering its head.

CREST The topmost part of a horse's neck between the poll, and the withers.

CRIBBER A horse that chews wood. A horse that bites into an object and sucks air into his lungs, also called a windsucker.

CRIBBING STRAP A device used to stop a horse from cribbing.

CROP A jockey's whip or bat.

CROSS (A) The manner in which a jockey holds the reins, one rein crosses the other. The jockey usually takes a cross as soon as he mounts a horse.

CROSS TIES Lines that are attached to a wall or post that snap to each side of a horse's halter to secure the horse.

CROUP	The upper part of the hindquarters from the loins to the base of the tail on a horse.
CRYPTORCHID	A horse that has not been castrated, yet has no testicles in his scrotum, they are still undecended.
CULL	A horse that has been regarded as poor and discarded or sold by an owner or breeder.
CUP HORSE	A distance running horse.
CUPPY TRACK	A surface on a racing strip, that breaks under the horse's hoofs.
CUP RACE	A race where the winner usually receives a cup, usually of gold or silver, in addition to the purse money.
CURBS	A ligament rupture on the back of the hock joint, which results in considerable swelling.
CURB STRAP	A strap or chain that passes under the lower jaw of a horse and is fastened to the bit. It is used to give the rider more leverage and control of a horse.
CURRY COMB	A rubber or metal device that is used to groom a horse.
CUSHION	The surface of the racing strip.

CUT	Besides the coventional definitions, it means to casterate a horse.
CUT DOWN	A horse struck by the shoes of another horse. Due to a bad stride a horse may cut himself down.
DAILY DOUBLE	A wager where you have to pick the winner of two successive races.
DAILY DOUBLE POOL	The total amount of money wagered on the Daily Double after all taxes and commissions are taken out.
DAILY RACING FORM	A newspaper which list all the horses that are scheduled to race on a particular day at a particular track. It also shows the past performances and a multitude of other information to aid horseplayers with their selections.
DAM	The mother of a horse.
DARK OR DARK DAY	A day there is no racing.
DARK HORSE	A horse that races a surprisingly strong race, and wins.
DAY MONEY	The daily money that a trainer charges a horse owner to train a horse. This figure varies depending on the trainer.

75

DAYS	A suspension by the stewards for an infraction of the rules.
DEAD HEAT	Two of more horses finishing a race at exactly the same time.
DEAD TRACK	When the racing surface of the track lacks resiliency.
DEAD WEIGHT	The weight that a horse has to carry in lead plates, to make up the weight difference between the combined weight of the jockey and saddle, and the weight that is assigned by the Racing Secretary. The jockey is considered live weight.
DEBUT	The first race that a horse races in.
DEBUTANTE	A term that usually refers to a two year old filly.
DECLARED	A horse that is withdrawn from a race in advance of scratch time.
DECLARED OUT	Same as Declared. To withdraw from a race in advance of scratch time.
DEEP FOOTING	The footing on certain parts of the racing surface; the footing is sometimes deeper alongside the rail, other times it is deeper when the strip is muddy or sloppy.

DERBY	A race for three year olds, whose owners pay a fee to enter, and an additional fee, to keep the horse entered in a race.
DESTROY	When a horse has to be humanely put to death because of injury.
DETENTION BARN	A structure that houses horses to check them for use of nonauthorized drugs.
DIRT TRACK	A race track that is a combination of sand and soil.
DISQUALIFIED	A horse may be disqualified from a certain position in a race for an infraction of the rules and placed down one or more places in the standings.
DISTAFF SIDE	The ancestry of a horse traced through female ancestors only.
DISTANCE	The amount of ground from the beginning to the end of a race.
DISTANCED	A horse that is more than 25 lengths behind the winner.
DISTANCE HORSE	A horse that usually runs in a longer race, usually a mile or longer.
DISTANCE OF GROUND	A distance of over a mile.

DISTANCE RACE	A race of a mile or more.
DIVISION	A race in which entrants must be divided, because there are too many horses entered to run at one time, usually in a Stake or Handicap race.
DO A HORSE UP	To treat a horses legs, then bandage the legs.
DOG	An uncomplimentary term used to describe a horse that doesn't show much ability or desire to win.
DOGS	Portable rails placed out from the rail to prevent horses, during workouts, from disturbing the footing along the rail.
DOLLAR ODDS	The profit a bettor receives on a successful bet of $1.00. To figure the dollar odds of a pay-off, subtract the amount wagered from the pay off and divide by two.
DOPE	A narcotic or other substance given to alter the running form of a horse. It can be used to make a horse run either faster or slower.
DOUBLE	Short for Daily Double.

DOUBLE CALL	When a jockey is named to ride two or more horses in the same race.
DOUBLE ENTRY	When an owner or trainer enters two of his horses in one race as a single entry, for betting purposes.
DOWN ON HIS	A horse whose pasterns are long or slope lower than they should be.
DOWN THE LANE	Down the stretch, the straightaway portion of the track that ends at the finish line.
DRAW CLEAR	A horse finishing a race while increasing the distance between it and the rest of the field.
DRAW IN	It is when a horse is on the also eligible list, and because of a scratch in the race, he is able to become a starter.
DRIVE	To urge, or whip a horse on with an all out effort, especially in the homestretch.
DRIVING	Urging a horse on strongly by his rider.
DROP	A mare giving birth to a foal.
DROPPED	When a horse or rider falls.
DROPPED IN CLASS	Entering a horse in a cheaper race than it normally was entered in.
DWELT	When a horse breaks late from the gates.

79

EARLY FOOT	Same as early speed. A horse that gets off to a fast start.
EARLY SPEED	A horse that takes the lead early in the race or challenges for it.
EARNINGS	The money a horse has won from purses.
EASED	A horse that is pulled up gently in a race, usually because it is sore or lame.
EASILY	A horse winning a race without being pressed by his rider or other opposition.
EIGHTH	A furlong or 220 yards, or 660 feet or 1/8th of a mile.
ELIGIBLE	A horse that is qualified according to the conditions set by the track, or the conditions of a race.
ENTER	To name a horse to compete in a race.
ENTRY	Two or more horses owned or trained by the same person running as a unit in the betting.
ENTRY CLERK	The employee of the race track that is responsible for accepting entries of horses in races.
ENTRY FEE	The money paid by an owner or trainer to start a horse in a special race.

EQUINE	Pertaining to a horse.
EQUIPMENT	Blinkers, saddle, etc. carried by a horse in a race.
EVEN MONEY	A wager that would return a profit equal to the amount wagered.
EXACTA	A wager where a bettor must name the first, and second place horse in the exact order of finish.
EXACTA POOL	The total amount of money wagered on the exacta after all taxes and commissions are taken out.
EXCUSED	This is when a horse is withdrawn from a race with the consent of the stewards.
EXERCISE BOY	A rider who exercises horses.
EXTENDED	When a horse is forced to run at top speed.
EXTENDED PARI-MUTUEL MEETING	A race meet, without an agricultural fair in progress, which last at least ten days and has pari-mutuel wagering.
EXTRA RACE	A race that is scheduled because the book race failed to draw sufficient entries.

EXTRAS

A list of races and conditions drafted by the Racing Secretary as a substitute for the races listed in the Condition Book.

EXTRA WEIGHT

More weight that the race conditions require.

FADE

A horse that is losing ground, especially in the stretch: tired and slowing down.

FALSE START

A start in which horses start before the Starters signal. This is impossible today with modern starting gates, with the exception of when a mechanical failure occurs and some of the gates do not open in a race.

FARRIER

A blacksmith, a person who shoes horses.

FAST TRACK

When the footing on the racing strip is at its best condition, dry, fast and even.

FAULTERED

A horse that stopped running before the end of the race, lacking stamina.

FAULTS

The weak points of a horse.

FAVORITE

The horse that is expected to win by the majority of the bettors.

FEATHER

Light weight.

FEATURE (THE)   Referring to the feature race or the most important race on the program.

FEATURE RACE   The most important race on the program for the day.

FEE'S   The amount paid to a jockey for riding a certain race, or the amount paid for entering a horse in a certain race.

FELL BACK   A horse that lacked stamina and stopped running before the end of the race.

FENCE   The outside rail of the racing surface.

FETLOCK   The joint joining the cannon bone to the pastern of a horse's leg.

FIELD   Due to the fact that pari-mutuel machines can only handle 12 betting units in each race, it becomes necessary to establish a field if a race has over 12 entries. These extra entries are all grouped together as a single betting unit. Because of the increased possiblity of winning, only longshots are placed in the field.

FILL   A race that does not fill is a race where there are not enough horses entered to substantiate the running of the race.

FILLY   A female horse up to and including four years of age.

83

FILM PATROL   A system whereby movies are taken from various locations around the track from different angles to insure that no infractions of rules happen during the race. These movies can be viewed by the stewards within minutes after the finish of the race in the case of an inquiry.

FINE   A penalty imposed for violating rules of racing.

FINGER HORSE   The horse favored to win, which is sometimes indicated on a scratch sheet by a hand with a pointing finger.

FIRING   The applying of a searing instrument to a horse's leg to promote healing of damaged fibres.

FIRST CALL   It is when a stable engages a jockey's services, either through a contract or mutuel agreement, whereby that stable has first claim on a jockey to ride their horse in a race. If a stable doesn't have a horse in a race, the jockey is free to ride any other horse in the race.

FIRST TURN   The first bend in the track beyond the starting point.

FIT   A horse's condition. A horse that is fit is in top condition and ready to race.

FLAG	The signal held by a man stationed a short distance in front of the starting gate at the exact starting point of the race.
FLAG MAN	The official who drops the flag to denote the start of the race.
FLASH	The lights on the tote board flash to show a change in odds in the betting on a race. The updating of the odds on the board happens many times before the start of the race. Each time the odds change, it is considered a flash.
FLAT RACE	A race on level ground with a jockey astride the horse.
FLATS	The same as flat race. Thoroughbred racing as we see to today.
FLAT SHOE	A flat shoe is flat on both sides.
FLATTEN OUT	When a horse in a race tires and his head drops almost on a straight line with its body.
FLIP	When a horse rears up on its hind legs and goes over backwards.
FLIPPER	A horse that is known to rear up on it's hind legs and go over backwards in the starting gates.

FLIPPER A person who makes money by flipping discarded pari-mutual tickets over to determine if any of them are winning tickets.

FLIPPING When a jockey voluntarily forces up food or liquid, to help control his weight.

FLOAT TEETH To file a horses teeth so they are not sharp, which aids digestion.

FLOAT THE TRACK To squeeze off surface water from the racing strip.

FOAL A newborn horse. A foal can be either a male or female. Also to give birth.

FOOT A term used to describe speed. A horse with early foot is a horse with early speed.

FOOTING The condition of the racing surface usually referring to the depth of the cushion.

FORM PLAYER A bettor who uses past performances and a horse's rated ability and other information usually listed in the Racing Form and other publications in considering wagers.

FORM The Daily Racing Form.

FORM	Term used to describe the condition of a horse, such as top form.
FOUL	It is when an owner, trainer or jockey files a protest. It is also called an inquiry.
FOUNDER	Also called laminitis. It is a congestion or inflamation in the horses feet.
FOUR FURLONGS	880 yards, 2640 feet, or a ½ of a mile. There are eight furlongs to a mile.
FRACTIONAL TIMES	The intermediate times attained in a race. They are taken at different points of the race.
FRACTIONS	Term used to discribe the fractional times.
FREE HANDICAP	A race in which no liability is incurred for entrance money until the acceptance of the assigned weight.
FREE LANCE	An independant rider not under contract.
FREEZE	A medication or treatment that deadens the nerves in a horse's legs to make it race without pain, thus enabling a sore horse to compete.
FRESHENING	To rest a horse from racing or training.

FROG	The triangular shaped pad in the middle of the sole of a horse's foot that acts as a cushion.
FRONT END	The horse that is in the lead in a race is said to be on the front end.
FRONT RUNNER	A horse that quickly takes the lead and sets the pace for the other horses in the race.
FURLONG	One eighth of a mile, 220 yards, or 660 feet.
FUTURITY	A race for two year old horses who's owners paid a fee to enter their horse, before it was born, and a fee to keep the horse in the race.
GAD	The rider's whip; also called a bat, crop, or stick.
GAIT	The manner in which a horse moves, walk, trot, gallop, etc.
GALLOP	A type of gait also called a canter.
GALLOP BOY	An exercise rider. A person who exercises horses.
GALLOP IN HAND	An extending canter but the horse remains collected, not a flat out run.

GAP	The opening on the track where the horses enter onto the racing strip.
GAS	The term gas is used the same as speed or power. A horse with a lot of gas, has a lot of speed. A horse that runs out of gas is a horse that loses power and gets tired.
GASKIN	A part of a horses hind leg between the thigh and the hock.
GATE	Refers to the total attendance at a track.
GATE CREW	The guys that lead the horses into the starting gates and help to calm unruly horse to insure the safety of the jockeys and also to try to insure an equal start for each horse in the race. Although they seldom receive the credit they deserve, they have one of the most important jobs on the race track.
GATES	The starting device or barrier.
GELDING	A male horse that has been castrated.
GESTATION PERIOD	The time from breeding to the delivery of the foal; usually eleven months and five days.
GET	The offspring of a stallion.

GET A CHECK   The money or portion of the purse that an owner receives because the horse finished in either of the first five positions in a race.

GETAWAY DAY   The last day of the race meet when trainers and other track people are leaving for other tracks.

GET THE ORDERS   When the jockey is told by the owner or trainer how he is to ride the horse in the race and other pertinent information about the horse.

GETTING DAYS   A suspension by the stewards for an infraction of the rules.

GET YOUR PICTURE TAKEN   To win the race.

GIMMICK RACE   Races in which you bet on a combination of horses such as the Quinella, Daily Double, or Tri-Fecta.

GIMPY   When a horse is slightly lame or sore.

GIRTH   The band that goes around the body of the horse to hold the saddle in place.

GIRTH RASH   A rash that a horse gets from having a dirty girth.

GIVE WEIGHT	When a horse is required to carry more weight in a race than his rivals.
GOGGLES	What a jockey wears to protect his eyes in a race.
GOING	A term used in referring to the condition of the track.
GOING AWAY	A horse that is increasing it's lead over other horses while winning a race.
GOING WIDE	A horse going outside the pack, away from the rail.
GOOD BOTTOM	When the track is firm under the surface.
GOOD DOER	A horse with a good appetite.
GOOD GATE BOY	A jockey who has the ability to consistently get a horse out of the gates fast, usually breaking on top, which gives a speed horse a definate advantage.
GOOD HANDS	A term used in referring to a jockey who utilizes his hands in a manner which helps a horse perform at its best.
GOOD MOUTH	A horse with a soft sensitive mouth that responds easily to the reins.
GOOD TRACK	It is the condition of the track when it is almost dry.

GO TO THE
FRONT   Take the lead in the race.

GRABBING HIS   It is when the toe of the hind shoe
QUARTER   strikes the foreleg on the heel. Also called over-reaching.

GRADED RACES Races where the horses are graded by the track handicappers' estimate.

GRADUATE   When a horse or rider wins their first race; also called breaking their maiden.

GRAND DAM   The grandmother of a horse.

GRAND SIRE   The grandfather of a horse.

GRAND SLAM   A grandslam is when a jockey wins every race on the program on a particular day. It is a rare feat.

GRAND STAND The principal structure used for spectators at a race course.

GRASS RACES Races that are run on a turf course.

GRAY   A color of a horse which has a mixture of white and black hairs.

GREEN HORSE A beginning or inexperienced horse. A horse that is just starting training.

GROOM   The person who takes care of horses in the stable area. He feeds, waters, brushes, and cares for the horse for the trainer.

GROUNDED   A jockey that is suspended from racing.

HALF   A half mile, four furlongs, 880 yards, or 2640 feet.

HALF BROTHER   A male horse's relationship to another horse that is out of the same dam but by a different sire.

HALF MILE POLE A distinctively colored vertical post usually painted red and white, that is inside the inside rail, one half mile from the finish line.

HALF-MILER   A race track that is one-half of a mile in circumference.

HALF ROUND SHOES These shoes are similar to a flat shoe with the exception of the surface that strikes the track, which is round.

HALF SISTER   A female horse out of the same dam but by different sires.

HALTER   A device used to control a horse when it is not being ridden. It attaches to a horse's head. It is similar to a bridle but it does not have a bit or reins.

HALTERMAN	A person who claims a horse.
HAND	A unit used in measuring the height of a horse. One hand is 4 inches.
HANDICAP	To evaluate horses in a race by their past preformances, distance of the race, weight carried, track conditions, rider, etc.
HANDICAPPER	A person who handicaps races either for a track or a publication, or for his own use.
HANDICAP RACE	A race in which the track handicapper assigns the weight a horse has to carry in the race.
HANDILY	Working or racing with a moderate effort, not under the whip.
HANDLE (mutuel)	The amount of money bet on a race, totally for the week, month, or the season.
HAND RIDE	Urging the horse with the hands, not by the use of the whip.
HARD BOOT	A Kentucky horseman.
HAT TRICK	When a jockey, owner, or trainer wins three consecutive races.

HAY	It is plant matter cut and dried for use as fodder. A horse eats approximately 10 lbs. of hay per day.
HAY BURNER	A disrespectful name for a horse.
HEAD	The unit of measurement used to describe the distance between horses in a race. It is equal to the length of the horse's head.
HEADED, (TO BE)	To be overtaken in a race or workout.
HEAD OF THE STRETCH	The beginning of the straight portion of track ending at the finish line.
HEART	A horse or rider that shows great determination and desire to win; courage.
HEAT	A race.
HEAVY HEADED	A horse that is difficult to control with the reins, that usually pulls against the bit and tends to run with his head low.
HEAVY TRACK	This is the condition of the track when it is drying out. It is the slowest of all conditions.
HEIGHT	The height of a horse is measured in hands, from the ground to a horses' withers. A hand is equal to four inches.

H.B.P.A.	The Horseman's Benevolent and Protective Association. An International organization of owners and trainers associated for the purpose of performing charitable works for it's members and other horsemen, and advancing their relationship with the controlling bodies of racing, race tracks, the public and government interest.
HELMET	A protective hat a jockey wears during a race or workout.
HIGH FLANKER	A horse with one or both testicles in the inguinal canal rather than the scrotum.
HIGH-NERVE	To nerve a horse above the knee or hock.
HIGH-WEIGHT	The horse that is assigned the highest weight to carry in a race.
HIP NUMBER	A number assigned to a horse so that it can be identified easily at a sale. A hip number is usually referred to when a horse is yet unnamed.
HIT	When a battery or joint is applied to a horse in a race or workout.
HIT A BRICK WALL	It is said of a horse that was racing well and suddenly stopped as if it had run into a brick wall.

96

HITTING THE BOX	It refers to a jockey going into the steam room to lose weight.
HOBBLE	To secure a horse's feet together to prevent it from kicking.
HOCK	A part of a horses rear leg between the gaskin and the cannon.
HOLD A HORSE	To restrain a horse from running its best.
HOLE	A space between horses or between a horse and the rail through which another horse can pass.
HOLE	Another name for a post position.
HOME BRED	A horse that is foaled in the same jurisdiction in which it is to race.
HOME STRETCH	It is the straightaway part of the track running from the last turn to the finish line.
HONEST	A horse that races according to the form that it has shown in prior races and workouts.
HOOF	The foot of a horse.
HOOF OINTMENT	A dressing used to keep the horse's foot from becoming brittle and cracking.

HOP   To give a horse forbidden drugs or narcotics.

HORSE   An equine animal. In racing it is also used to describe a male horse five years old or older, that has not been casterated.

HORSE PLAYER   A person who bets or plays the horses.

HORSE RACING   The racing of Thoroughbred horses, against each other over an oval track. Horse racing today is the number one major spectator sport in the United States. This is mainly due to pari-mutual betting.

HOSTLER   A name for a groom.

HOT BOX   Another name for the steam room the jockeys use to lose weight.

HOT HORSE   A term used to describe a horse after a workout or a race before it is cooled off. Also refers to a horse that has an expected amount of money wagered on it.

HOTS   A term used to describe horses after a workout or a race before they are cooled off.

HOTWALK   To walk a horse until it is cooled.

HOT WALKER	A person who walks a horse to cool it out; also a machine which walks a horse around in a circle.
HUNCH PLAYER	A bettor who relies on some immaterial fact or circumstance to guide him in his wager on a race.
HUNG	A horse that is tired but holding on to a position.
ICE	Putting a horse's legs in buckets of ice or boots filled with ice, or to apply ice packs to a horse's legs to help deaden pain.
IDENTIFIER	The person that is responsible for the identifications of all horses coming into the paddock, which includes checking the tattoo number, color, markings, etc.
IMPEDE	To check, retard or hinder the progress of another horse.
IMPOST	The weight a horse carries.
INFIELD	The part of the race track that is encircled by the racing strip.
IN FOAL	Pregnant. A mare is considered in foal when she is pregnant.

99

IN HAND	When a jockey is holding back a horse to reserve some of its speed.
INQUIRY	When the stewards are examining a claim of foul.
INSIDE FREEZE	A freeze that is injected internally.
INSIDE RAIL	The rail or fence that runs around the racing strip closest to the infield.
INSTRUCTIONS	When the owner or trainer gives the orders to the jockey as to how he wants the horse ridden in the race.
INTERMEDIATE	A race is considered an intermediate distance if the race is between 7 furlongs and 1 1/8 miles long.
IN THE MONEY	A horse that finishes in the first five positions in a race. Purse money is usually divided between the first five finishers. From a betting standpoint it is a horse that finishes in the first three positions in the race due to the fact that pari-mutuel betting only pays off for those positions.
INVITATIONAL RACE	A race in which the horses are selected and then their owners are invited to enter them.

IRON JAW	Referring to a horse that has a tough mouth, that does not respond to the bit and is hard to control, often running off with it's rider.
IRONS	The stirrups.
JOCKETTE	A girl jockey.
JOCKEY	A person who rides a horse in a race.
JOCKEY AGENT	The person who arranges the mounts, and other business for a jockey.
JOCKEY COLONY	It refers to the complete group of jockeys racing at a particular track.
JOCKEY CLUB, THE	The registry of Thoroughbreds. All Thoroughbreds racing on the North American Continent must be registered with the Club and their names approved by them.
JOCKEY GUILD	An organization for jockeys.
JOCKEY ROOM	A room where the jockey dresses and waits for the races he is to ride.
JOCKEY ROOM CUSTODIAN	The jockey room custodian is in charge of the jockey room and all the equipment therein, including all colors, and the personal equipment of all the jockeys.

101

JOG	A slow easy gait.
JOINT	An illegal device used to prod a horse, also called a battery, machine, or short stick.
JOURNEYMAN	A jockey that has completed an apprenticeship.
JUDGE	The stewards are the judges. There are also Associate Judges which include the Paddock Judge, Patrol Judge, Barrier Judge, etc.
JUG	A bottle of liquid vitamins and electrolytes that is given to a horse the day before the race.
JUGHEAD	An uncomplementary term some use in referring to a Standardbred horse.
JUMPED UP	A horse that unexpectedly ran a big race and won is said to have jumped up and won the race.
JUVENILE	A two year old horse.
KENTUCKY DERBY	A stakes race for 3 year old Thoroughbred racehorses over a 1¼ mile course, held annually at Churchhill Downs Race Track, Louisville, Kentucky. It is the first race of the Thoroughbred Triple Crown.

KENTUCKY OAKS	A stakes race for three-year old fillies exclusively.
KITCHEN	Same as track kitchen, which is a restaurant on the backstretch for horsemen and other track personnel.
KNEE SPAVIN	A bony growth at the back of a horse's knee on the inner side.
LAME	A sore or injured horse.
LAMINITIS	A inflamation of the sensitive part under the horney wall of a horses hoof.
LANE	Another name for the stretch, or the straightaway portion of the track that ends at the finish line.
LAP	The complete circumference of an oval-shaped race track. Once around the track.
LASIX	A diuretic that helps prevent horses from bleeding.
LATCH	Another name for the starting gates.
LAY	To stay in a certain position during a race, an example is when a jockey is told to lay in fourth position until the stretch run.

LAY OFF	It is when a bookmaker has accepted more bets than he is comfortable with and decides to lay off or wager some of them through the pari-mutual windows or with other bookmakers, to try to avoid possible loss.
LAY OFF	To give a horse time off from racing to let it rest.
LEAD	To take the lead or go to the front in the race.
LEADS	A horse leads with one leg or the other and must be taught to change leads in order to race on an oval track.
LEAD PAD	The pad placed under the saddle that is used to carry lead weights.
LEAD PONY	The horse that leads the race horse and jockey from the paddock to the starting gate at the beginning of the race.
LEAD SHANK	A strap that attaches to the halter to lead a horse.
LEAD WEIGHTS	Bars of lead that are carried in the lead pads, to make up the difference in weight between the actual weight of the jockey and the weight the horse is assigned to carry in the race.

104

LEAKY ROOF CIRCUIT — A term used to describe a minor track or bush track.

LEASE — The loaning or renting of a horse by the legal owner to another person for the purpose of either racing or breeding.

LEATHERS — Leather straps that connect the jockeys' stirrup irons to the saddle.

LEFT BEHIND — A horse that is late breaking from the gate.

LEG UP (A Horse) — To condition a horses' legs by exercise.

LEG UP — To give a jockey a hand getting up on a horse.

LENGTH — The distance between the front and back of a horse, usually about eight feet. The unit of measurement used to describe the distance between horses in a race.

LICENSE — All track personnel whether they are owners, trainers, grooms, etc. must be licensed by the Racing Commission that has jurisdiction in the State they are working.

LIKES THE TRACK — When a horse does particularly well on a certain race track.

LIMBER UP	To stretch a horse's muscles by exercising before a race.
LINE	In breeding it refers to horses traceable to a common paternal ancestor.
LIVE WEIGHT	The weight of the jockey, as opposed to dead weight, or the lead weights that are carried in the lead pads. Most trainers feel it is better to carry live weight than for the horse to carry lead to make up the difference in the assigned weights.
LOAFER	A horse that must be continually urged to race at its best, by its jockey.
LOCK	A horse that is a sure winner in a particular race.
LONG SHOT	A horse with very little money bet on it. A horse not favored to win a race.
LOSE AN IRON	When a jockey's foot comes out of the stirrup.
LOOSE RIDER	A jockey that rides reckless and does not watch where he is going. When a jockey is charged by the stewards of reckless riding he is often fined and suspended.
LOOSE MOUNT	A horse that has unseated its rider in a race.

LOW-NERVE   A horse that is nerved below the knee or hock.

LUG   When a horse bears in or out.

LUNGE   A horse rearing or plunging.

LUNGE   Working a horse around in a circle with a rope or line connected to it's halter.

LUNGE LINE   A rope or line approximately 20 to 25 feet long that connects to a horse's halter and is used to lunge a horse.

MACHINE   Another name for an illegal device used to prod a horse, also called a joint, a buzzer, or a battery.

MACHINES   It refers to the pari-mutuel machines.

MAIDEN   A horse or jockey that has never won a race.

MAIDEN MARE   A mare that has never had a foal even though she may be carrying one.

MAIDEN RACE   A race that features horses that have never won a race.

MAKE A BID   When a horse makes a move or challenge in a race.

MANE	The long hair on the neck of a horse. The jockey sometimes holds on to the mane of the horse when he comes out of the gate.
MARE	A female horse over the age of five years old.
MARKINGS	The white body coloration on a horse such as star, snip, stockings, etc.
MATCH RACE	A race between two horses to determine which is best.
MATURITY	A race for 4 year olds who were entered for the race before they were foaled.
MEDICATION LIST	A list that tells what medication a horse has taken for a race. In some States medication is not allowed.
MEET	The racing days at a track, also called the race meet.
MIDSTRETCH	A position approximately between the eighth-pole and the finish line.
MILLION (THE)	A stakes race that originated at Arlington Park, featuring horses that are considered the best in the world, competing for a million dollar purse, sponsored by Budweiser Beer.

MINUS POOL A situation that occasionally develops in betting when so much money is bet on one horse that the balance of the pool is insufficient to pay off the minimum amount of money required by state law. The track has to make up the deficit.

MINUTE BOOK A book that is maintained by the stewards that records all complaints and investigation and the disposition and findings of them.

MONEY LINES The amount of money a horse has won. The horses record for his most recent two years, including the number of starts, wins, etc.

MORNING GLORY A horse that runs real well in the morning workouts, but does not run well in the races in the afternoon.

MORNING LINES The approximate odds quoted at the track on the morning of the race, after the scratches and track conditions are known.

MORNING TELEGRAPH (THE) A daily newspaper that reports in detail the past performances of horses racing, as well as the results from past races and other racing information.

MOUNT The horse that a jockey is to ride in a race is a jockey's mount.

MOUNT MONEY	This is the money the jockey is paid for riding a horse in a race.
MOVED UP	To step a horse up in class to a higher caliber race than it normally has been racing in.
MOVIE LIST	A list of compiled by the Stewards of Jockeys required to attend the reviewing of previous days races for possible infractions of the rules.
MOVIES	Refers to the movies or films of the races that are taken while the races are in progress.
MUCK OUT A STALL	To clean out a stall.
MUCK TUBS	A device used to carry manure and old bedding out from a stall, while cleaning it.
MUDDER	A horse that runs well on an off track.
MUDDY TRACK	A track condition is muddy when it is soft all the way through.
MUDLARK	A horse that delights in running on a muddy or soft track.
MUD MARKS	Symbols used to show if a horse is a fair, good, or superior mud runner.

MUTUEL FIELD   Same as Field: A group of entries grouped together as a single betting unit.

MUTUEL POOL   Same as the betting pool, the total
amount of money bet on any race, or for
a particular day of racing.

MUZZLE   A device that fits over the nose and
mouth of a horse to prevent it from biting
people or other horses. It is also used to
prevent a horse from eating before a
race.

NAMED   When a trainer tells who the jockey is
that is assigned to ride a horse in a race.
When you see No-Boy on an entry or in
a publication it means that the trainer
hasn't yet named the jockey that is to
ride the horse.

NAPE   The top of the neck of a horse also
called the poll.

N.A.S.R.C   The National Association of State
Racing Commissioners. It's members
consist of members of Racing Commis-
sions or Racing Boards in the United
States, Canada, Mexico, Puerto Rico, the
Bahamas, etc.

**NAVICULAR
BONE**   A bone in a horses foot.

NAVICULAR DISEASE	A corrosive ulcer on the navicular bone of a horses foot.
NEAR SIDE	The left side of a horse.
NECK	The unit of measurement used to describe the distance between horses in a race. The unit is usually the distance or length of a horses neck, usually about four feet.
NECK AND NECK	When two or more horses are racing along side of each other.
NEED A RACE	A term that is used to describe a horse that has not yet reached it's peak condition, yet is in a race to get it in better racing condition. Some trainers hold the contention that a race is better than three workouts, while other trainers will not start a horse until they feel it is able to win.
NERVED	An operation that cuts vital nerves to enable a horse to race without pain.
NEURECTOMY	Same as nerved. An operation that cuts or removes vital nerves to enable a horse to race without pain.
NIGHTCAP	The last race for the day.

NIGHT EYE   Another name for the chestnut, which is a horny growth on the inside of a horses' leg.

NIPPERS   A tool that is used in trimming horses hoofs.

NO-BOY   On an entry or publication where a jockey is normally listed it means, that the trainer hasn't named the jockey that is to ride his horse in the race.

NOD   When a horse wins a race by lowering it's head.

NOMINATE   To name a horse to race in a specific race well in advance of the race, sometimes even before a horse is foaled.

NOMINATOR   The person who nominates a horse for a future race.

NOSE   The distance or advantage of one horse over another, which is approximately the length of a horses nose. Usually a photo decides the winner.

NOSEBAND   The lower band that passes over the nose of a horse and attaches to the cheek strap on the bridle of a horse.

NOSE BET   A wager that is placed on a horse to WIN.

113

NOT FIT	When a horse is not in top condition.
NUMBER CLOTH	The cloth that is placed under the saddle of a horse that denotes the starting position of the horse, and is visible so viewers can see where a particular horse is running in a race.
OATS	A cereal crop that is used as the main ingredient of the various grains that are fed to a horse. It is fed either whole, crimped or crushed.
OBJECTION	The claim of foul lodged by the jockey, trainer or the owner of the horse.
OBJECTION SIGN	The sign that is displayed on the tote board that lights up when a claim of foul is lodged. The race is not official until the Stewards determine if a foul was committed.
ODDS	The percentages or chances of a horse winning a race.
ODDS BOARD	Also called the tote board. It displays the odds, along with a multitude of other information.
ODDS ON	The favorite horse. The odds on this horse are less than even money.

OFF	Started. When the announcer says "And they're off" it means that the race has started.
OFF	Sore or not normal. A jockey may tell a trainer that a horse is a little off in the right front, which means, the horse is either sore or has some problem with that particular leg.
OFF BELL	The bell that rings signifying the start of the race and the closing of pari-mutuel wagering. Also called the starting bell and the closing bell.
OFF FORM	A horse that is not racing as his past performance charts would indicate.
OFFICIAL	A person in charge, such as a Racing Official. A sign displayed when the results of a race are OFFICIAL.
OFFICIAL SIGN	The sign on the totalizator board that lights up when the race is declared "OFFICIAL". No tickets should be discarded until the race is "OFFICIAL".
OFF IT'S FEED	A horse that is not eating properly.
OFF SIDE	The right side of a horse.
OFF THE BOARD	When the odds on a horse are over 99-1; odds over this amount will not be shown. The board will remain at 99-1.

OFF THE PACE	When a horse comes from behind the leaders to win a race.
OFF TRACK	Any other condition of the race track other than a fast track.
OFF TRACK BETTING	Betting establishments, that handle pari-mutuel wagering, that are controlled by the State, and are set up at various off track locations so that people that are unable or unwilling to go to the track can still place their bets.
ONE FOR THE BOY	A win ticket that is bought for a jockey by an owner or trainer and given to the jockey before the start of the race to try to induce the jockey to put an extra effort into winning the race.
ON ITS TOES	It is said of a horse that is feeling good, in peak condition, and is eager to race.
ON THE BIT	When the horse is pulling on the reins or is eager to run.
ON THE BOARD	When a horse finishes in one of the top four positions of the race.
ON THE CUFF	When something is purchased on credit to be paid at a later time.
ON THE FRONT END	It refers to the horse racing in the lead, or the horse that won the race.

ON THE NOSE   To bet a horse to WIN.

ON THE RAIL   A horse running close to the rail, which is the shortest distance around the track.

ON THE WOOD   A term describing the inside rail.

ON TOP   Same as First; the horse that breaks on top is the first horse out of the gates.

OPEN AT   The odds of a horse when it is first placed on the tote board, the first flash.

OPEN COMPANY   It refers to the horses in a race who's entries are not limited to statebred horses.

OPENER   The first race of the day.

OPEN MOUNT   A horse that is entered in a race but does not have a Jockey named to ride it.

OPEN RACE   A race in which all horses can compete.

ORAL SYRINGE   A device used to administer liquid medicine orally to a horse.

OSSELETS   A bony growth on a horses fetlock or ankle joint that is caused by inflammation of the bone membranes, which were caused by injuries such as wounds, sprains, bruises, etc.

OTB   Off track betting.

OUCHY	A term used to describe a horse that is sore or lame.
OUTCLASSED	When a horse beats it opposition so decisively as to appear far superior.
OUTFIT	A term that refers to a trainer and all his employees and equipment.
OUTLAW	A horse that is particularly mean and vicious.
OUT OF	In regards to breeding it indicates the mother of a horse.
OUT OF THE MONEY	Not finishing in the first three places as far as betting.
OUTRIDER	The person who leads the post parade and helps to stop horses after the race, or during a race in an emergency.
OUTSIDE FREEZE	A freeze that is applied externally to a horse to help deaden pain.
OUTSIDER	A horse that is a longshot and is not expected to win the race.
OUTSTANDING TICKET	A winning pari-mutuel ticket that has not been redeemed.
OVAL	Another name for a race track.

OVERDUE	A horse that should have won previous races and is expected to win in the near future.
OVER IT'S HEAD	To run a horse in a race where all the other horses are far superior.
OVERLAND	When a jockey takes the horse to the outside or around the other horses. It is the longest way to the finish line.
OVERLAY	An overlay is when a horses chances of winning are greater than the odds on the tote board indicate.
OVERLAY	The same as a minus pool. A situation that occasionally develops in betting when so much money is bet on one horse that the balance of the pool is insufficient to pay off. The track makes up the difference.
OVERMATCHED	A horse that is racing against far superior horses.
OVERNITE LINE	The odds quoted right before the race.
OVERNIGHT RACE	A race that closes entries 72 hours or less before the post time for the first race on the day the race is scheduled.

OVERNIGHTS	The schedule of horses and jockeys named to ride them, that is put out by the Racing Secretary, after all the entries are gathered.
OVER REACHING	It is when the toe of the hind hoof strikes the fore leg on the heel.
OVERWEIGHT	When a jockey's actual riding weight, including his equipment, exceeds the weight officially assigned to his mount.
OWNER'S AUTHORIZED AGENT	The person authorized by the owner of a horse to represent him on official racing business.
PACE	The speed or running style of a horse in a race.
PACK (THE)	The horses that are racing in a group behind the leaders.
PADDOCK	The area where the horses are saddled and kept just before post time.
PADDOCK JUDGE	The official who is in charge of the paddock, who inspects all horses and equipment prior to each race.
PAPER TRAINER	A trainer that supplies a stall and the use of his name, etc., to an individual who is actually training, feeding and caring for the horse, but does not have a valid trainers license.

PARI-MUTUELS ODDS	The odds that are paid on winning bets at a pari-mutuel track.
PARI-MUTUELS	The form of betting and of handling the betting, on horse racing at the race track.
PARI-MUTUEL TICKET	The receipt the bettor receives, showing the terms of the bet.
PARLAY	To bet an original amount, plus it's winnings on a subsequent race.
PASTEBOARD TRACK	A track with a lightning-fast racing strip.
PASTERN	The bone in a horse's leg between the fetlock and the coronet or the area around it.
PAST PER-FORMANCES	A chart that shows how a horse ran in the past. It usually shows the horse's last ten races.
PAST POSTING	To bet a horse with the bookmaker after the race is over and the horse has won. This is sometimes possible due to time errors.
PATROL JUDGES	The Officials who observe the progress of a race from various vantage points around the racing strip.
PAY OFF	The amount of money that is to be returned on a winning bet.

121

PEDIGREE	It is a chart recording a line of ancestors, also called a family tree.
PENALTIES	Extra weight a horse has to carry according to the conditions of the race.
PERFECTA	A race where a bettor must name the first and second place horses in the exact order of finish, also called the EXACTA.
PHOTO	A photo is taken at the finish of every race as the winning horse crosses the finish line. When necessary this photo is used to determine the order of finishing the race.
PHOTO FINISH	When a photo is used to determine the winner of a race.
PIC 6	A wager where you must select the winners of six successive races. Same as Big 6 or Sweep 6.
PICK ITS HEAD UP	When a horse is tiring it tends to lower its' head, a good jockey is able to pick its' head up and get a final effort from the horse.

PICTURE

The picture refers to either of two pictures; one is the picture taken as the horse crosses the finish line; the other is when the horse and jockey return to the winner circle to get their picture taken with the owner, trainer, groom, etc., to celebrate the winning of the race.

PINCHED

When a horse is forced to slow down slightly because the hole or space he is trying to go through is not sufficient.

PINCHED BACK

When a horse is in close quarters in a race and forced back.

PIN-FIRED

To use a searing instrument on a horse's leg to promote healing of damaged fibers.

PIN HEAD

An uncomplimentary name for a jockey.

PIPE OPENER

It is when a horse is exercised at a moderate speed.

PLACE

When you bet a horse to PLACE, you are betting that the horse will come in at least in second place. The horse must either win the race or finish in second place for you to collect your bet.

PLACE BET

A wager that a horse will come in second place in a race. If a horse finishes first or second you would win your bet if you bet a horse to Place.

123

PLACE MONEY   The money or portion of the purse that an owner of a horse would receive because the horse finished in second place. It is also the payoff on a Place Bet.

PLACE POOL   The total amount of money wagered to place on a particular race, after all commissions and taxes are deducted.

PLACE TICKET   A pari-mutuel ticket or wager that a horse will finish in Second Place in a race. If a horse finishes in First or Second Place you would win your bet with a PLACE TICKET.

PLACING JUDGE   The official who determines the order of finish of the horses in the race.

PLATER   A horse that races in claiming races.

PLATES   Lightweight racing shoes.

PLATTER   A person who puts shoes on a horse. Also called a farrier or blacksmith.

PLAY   To bet or wager on a horse race.

PLAY THE FAVORITES   A bettor or betting system whereby the bettor bets consistently on the horses favored to win the race.

PLUG   A slow horse, sometimes aged or unsound.

PLUG IN   To shock a horse with an illegal device, which is sometimes called a battery or joint.

POCKET   When a horse is boxed in or running in a position with horses in front and alongside.

POLE   A marker at measured distances around the track, ¼ pole, etc.

POLL   The topmost part of a horses head between its ears.

PONY   The horse that leads the race horse and jockey from the paddock to the starting gate at the beginning of the race. It is also a term used to describe the exercising of a horse while it is being lead by another horse.

PONY RIDER   The person who rides the pony while leading the other horses.

POOL   The money bet on an entire field of horses to WIN, PLACE, or SHOW.

POSITIVE TEST When a post-race test shows the presents of illegal drugs, whether they are stimulants, depressants, or seditives.

POST   The starting gate.

125

POST PARADE This is when the horses are paraded past the stands on their way to the starting gate.

POST POSITION The position in the starting gate from which a horse starts a race.

POST TIME The designated time for a race to start.

PREAKNESS STAKES A 1 3/16 mile stakes race for 3 year old racehorses that is held annually at Pimlico Race Track in Maryland. It is the second race of the Thoroughbred Triple Crown.

PREFER A horseman must specify one horse which he prefers, when entering more than one horse in a race.

PREFERRED LIST A list of horses with prior rights to start for various reasons.

PREP RACE A race in which a horse is entered to condition or prepare it for a more important race. A tune-up or trial race.

PRICE The amount of money that a horse paid or would have paid had he won.

PRODUCE The offspring of a mare.

PRODUCER A mare is considered a producer, when one of her sons or daughters has won a race.

PRODUCE RACE A race in which the contestants are the foals, of horses named at the time of entry.

PROGRAM A publication sold each day of racing at the track, which list information and lineups of each race. It includes information on the owner, trainer, jockey, morning odds, post position, sex, age, sire, dam, conditions of race, etc.

PROP When a horse stops suddenly by planting its front feet in the ground.

PROTEST The claim of foul lodged by the jockey, trainer, or owner. Same as Objection.

PUBLIC STABLE The stable of horses that are trained by a public trainer.

PUBLIC TRAINER A Trainer who accepts horses to train from anyone for a fee.

PULLED IT (He) A jockey who kept his mount from finishing in the money.

PULLED OUT A horse that is taken out toward the center of the track in an effort to pass horses in front of him.

PULLERS	Horses that pull against the bit when a jockey tries to restrain them. When a jockey cannot restrain a horse, it is hard to rate the horse so that it will have enough energy for a final effort in the stretch.
PULL UP	To stop a horse because of soreness or injury.
PURSE	The money received by the owner as a prize for a race.
PUT DOWN	A term used to describe a suspension in regards to a jockey. In regards to a horse; it means to humanely destroy the horse.
QUARTER	One quarter of a mile. 440 yards, 1320 feet.
QUARTER BOOTS	Boots used to protect a horse from overreaching.
QUARTER CRACK	A crack or verticle split found in the wall of the hoof which is caused from a dry or brittle hoof on improper shoeing.
QUARTER HORSE	A breed of horse, that gets its name because of it's racing ability over a race course ¼ of a mile long.
QUARTER POLE	A red and white marker one quarter of a mile from the finish line.

QUEEN'S PLATE	1¼ mile stakes race for 3 year old Canadian-bred racehorses. It is the oldest and most important horse race in Canada.
QUINELLA	A gimmick race in which you must pick the first two horses to cross the finish line, regardless of the order in which they finish.
QUINELLA POOL	The total amount of money wagered on the Quinella after all taxes and commissions are deducted.
QUITS	When a horse lacks stamina and stops racing before the end of the race.
QUITTER	A horse that lacks stamina and stops running before the end of the race.
RACE	A competition of two or more horses to determine a winner.
RACE COURSE	A race track which is properly constructed to conduct racing.
RACEHORSE	A Thoroughbred horse that is trained for racing on an oval track.
RACE MEETING	The racing days that are established for the purpose of holding a fixed number of races.
RACE RIDER	Another name for a jockey.

129

RACE TRACK An oval track on which horses compete to determine which is the fastest.

RACE TRACKER A person who frequents a race track.

RACE TRACK OPERATOR Any person, association, or corporation licensed by the State Racing Board to conduct horse racing within a States' jurisdiction.

RACING BAT A jockey's crop or whip. Also called a stick.

RACING BOARD The governing body that is responsible for regulating and supervising racing within a certain jurisdiction.

RACING CALENDAR A calendar established by the racing board that lists dates of race meetings, stake races and other dates pertaining to racing in a certain jurisdiction.

RACING COMMISSION A State Commission that regulates and controls racing in the State.

RACING FORM A newspaper which list all the horses that are scheduled to race on a particular day at a particular track. It also shows the past performances and a multitude of other information to aid horseplayers with their selections.

RACING PLANT Another name for a race track.

RACING PLATE	A horseshoe that is much thinner and lighter than a normal horseshoe.
RACING ROOM	When the horse, and the rider has sufficient space to exert the best efforts possible without being impeded by other horses in the race.
RACING SADDLE	A light weight saddle weighing as little as 12 oz. that is used as a rigging to hold the stirrup irons.
RACING SEAT	The way a jockey positions himself in the saddle during a race.
RACING SECRETARY	The Official who drafts the conditions for races and is responsible for the handling of entries and all other matters concerning the racing program. It is his job to try to insure the proper number of horses are running in each race.
RACING SOUND	A horse that is in sound condition and fit, while racing.
RACING STRIP	The actual race track or course.
RACING WIDE	A horse that is racing towards the outside fence rather than by the rail.
RAIL	The fence that separates the infield from the racing strip.

RAILBIRD	A person who stands along the rail in the mornings to watch the morning workouts.
RAIL RUNNER	A horse that likes to run along the rail.
RAKE OFF	That part of the money that is deducted from the pari-mutuel pools by the race track and the State, before any payments are made to individual bettors.
RALLY	When a horse seems to acquire fresh strength to finish a race.
RANK	An unwilling or tough horse.
RAN UP THE TRACK	A horse that runs a bad race and gave a poor showing of itself, finishing way out of the money.
RASP	A coarse file used in trimming horses hoofs.
RATE-A-HORSE	When a jockey times a horse so that he has enough energy for a final run at the end of the race.
REAR	When a horse stands up on its hind legs.
RECEIVING BARN	A structure that houses horses shipped in for a certain race. It is sometimes called an isolation barn.

RECORD	The fastest time in which a race has been conducted on a certain track for a specific distance.
REFUSE	When a horse will not break from the gate.
REGISTER	To record a horse's existence and to select a name to be approved by The Jockey Club.
REGISTRATION CERTIFICATE	The document which shows that a horse is registered with The Jockey Club (New York).
REINS	Long straps that are part of the bridle, that connect to the bit, that the jockey uses to steer and control a horse.
REINSMAN	Another name for a jockey.
RE-SET	When a horse is re-set, it's feet are trimmed, and it's old shoes are placed back on him.
RE-SHOD	When a horse is re-shod, it's feet are trimmed and new shoes replace the old ones.
RESTRICTED RACE	Races that are not for open company.

RETIRE TO STUD	When a stallion is withdrawn from racing and is used exclusively for breeding.
RIDDEN OUT	A horse finishing the race with the jockey urging him to the utmost.
RIDER	Another name for a jockey.
RIDGLING	A male horse with one or both organs of reproduction undescended. Also called a flanker.
RIDING INSTRUCTIONS	When the owner or trainer gives the orders to the jockey as to how he is expected to ride a horse in a race.
RIDING SHORT	The term is referring to a jockey who rides with short stirrups. Some trainers believe the longer the stirrup, the better the perch, but many jockeys feel that riding short is an advantage especially breaking from the gates on a speed horse.
RIGHT WAY	To go around the track counter clockwise, or in the same direction as in a race.
RINGBONE	A bony enlargement at the top of a horse's hoof on or near the pastern.
RINGER	A horse that is entered in a race under a false name.

134

RINGS   A device used while exercising a horse, to restrain it, so it doesn't run off.

ROARER   A horse that is breathing noisily.

ROGUE   An ill-mannered or ill-tempered horse who is unpredictable.

ROMP   A horse running with utmost ease. An easy win.

ROOM (The)   Another name for the jockey's room. A room where the jockey dresses and waits for the races he is to ride.

ROUTER   A horse that runs it's best in a race that is over a mile in distance.

ROUTES   Races that are over a mile long.

RULED OFF   To forbid an individual or horse from racing or from entering any race tracks controlled by a particular racing authority.

RUN DOWN   A horse with weak pasterns that scrape the ground while racing, is a horse that runs down.

RUNNER   A person who acts as a messenger and makes bets and cashes winning tickets for patrons at a track.

RUNNER	A Thoroughbred Race Horse that competes in races, also refers to a horse that has a lot of ability as a race horse.
RUNNING WIDE	A horse running outside the pack, away from the rail.
RUN OFF	While trying to gallop a horse, it runs at full speed with the jockey having little or no control over it.
RUN OFF THE FARM	A trainer that does not keep his horses at the race track. He brings them into the track when they are to race.
RUN OUT	When a horse runs toward the outer rail. Also refers to a horse running out of the money.
RUN OUT BIT	A bit used to control a horse from veering in or out while racing.
SADDLE	A seat for a jockey on the back of a horse.
SADDLE CLOTH	A cloth used under the saddle with a number denoting the horses post position.
SALIVA TEST	The testing of saliva from a horse after a race to determine if the horse had received any illegal drugs.

SALUTE	The acknowledgement given by a jockey to the racing official as he returns to the winner circle. It is followed by a sign given by the official for the jockey to dismount and weigh in.
SAVAGE	A horse biting another horse or a man.
SAVE GROUND	When a jockey keeps it's horse as close to the rail as possible during the race. Racing along the rail is the shortest way around the track.
SCALE OF WEIGHTS	A chart that determines the weights that horses are to carry, depending on the distance of the race, the sex, and age of the horse, and the month in which the race is run.
SCENIC ROUTE	The course that is followed when a horse races far from the inside rail.
SCHOOL	To train a horse to race, to be obedient and responsive to a riders commands, break properly from the gate, and to change leads when necessary while racing.
SCHOOLING LIST	A list of horses required by the Starter to undergo gate education.
SCORE	It refers to money won as a result of placing a successful bet.

SCORE A DOUBLE	When a jockey or trainer win two races in the same day.
SCRATCH	To take or withdraw a horse from a race.
SCRATCH SHEET	A publication showing the entries, scratches, selections, jockey, weight to be carried, type of race, probable odds, and other information, for the days races at one or more tracks.
SCRATCH TIME	The time of day in which all horses that are to be withdrawn from a race are officially withdrawn. All trainers with horses remaining in the race, must name their jockeys at this time. Jockeys are also required to acknowledge and check their mounts.
SEAT	The manner in which a jockey sits a horse.
SECOND CALL	To engage a jockey to ride when his contract commitment permits.
SECOND DAM	Grandmother or granddam.
SELLER	A person employed by the race track to sell pari-mutuel tickets.
SEND HIM	To urge the horse to take the lead early in the race.

138

SERVICE	The mating or breeding of a mare by a stallion.
SET DOWN	A term used to describe a jockey's suspension.
SET THE PACE	It is when a jockey takes his horse to the front in a race and rates his horse, thus determining how fast each fraction is timed in.
SEVEN FURLONGS	Seven eighths of a mile. 1540 yards, 4620 feet.
SEX ALLOWANCE	An allowance that a filly receives as a concession when running against males. Usually 3 to 5 pounds.
SHADOW ROLL	A sheepskin that is placed just below the eyes of a horse in order to prevent him from seeing moving shadows.
SHANK	A strap that attaches to a halter to lead a horse.
SHAPE	A term that is used to describe the condition of a horse.
SHEATH	The fold of flesh that contains the genital organ of a male horse.
SHED ROW	The stable area.

SHIN BUCKED	An inflamation of the cannon bone of a young horse with unseasoned legs.
SHOE	A plate put on the foot of a horse to protect it.
SHOE BOARD	A display that shows the different kinds of horseshoes worn by the horses in a race.
SHOEING	The actual act of putting shoes on a horse. Normally a horse should be re-shod or re-set approximately every four weeks.
SHOOT THE GAP	When a horse tries to turn off at the entrance of the track.
SHORT	A horse that tires before the end of the race. A horse that might have been leading, up until the last furlong, and then dropped back is a good example of a horse that is a little short. A horse that is not quite in top condition.
SHORT	Referring to racing a distance of less than a mile.
SHORT PRICE	When a horse is so heavily favored to win, that upon winning, it returns a minimal amount on a bet.
SHORT STICK	Another name for an illegal electrical device.

SHOT	A chance; as in a shot to WIN.
SHOW	When you bet a horse to SHOW, you are betting that the horse will come in at least in third place. The horse must finish the race in first, second or third place for you to collect your bet.
SHOW BET	A wager that a horse will finish in third place in the race. If a horse finishes in first, second, or third place in the race you would win your bet if you bet the horse to SHOW.
SHOW MONEY	The money or portion of the purse that an owner of a horse would receive because the horse finished in third place. It is also the payoff on a show bet.
SHOW POOL	The total amount of money wagered to Show on a particular race, after commissions and taxes are deducted.
SHOW TICKET	A pari-mutuel ticket or wager that a horse will finish in third place in the race. If a horse finishes in first, second, or third place, in the race you would win your bet if you bet the horse to show.
SHUT OFF	To cut off or cut in front of a horse in a race.

SHUT OUT	Not being able to place your bet before the start of the race.
SHY	Referring to a situation when a horse suddenly swerves away from an obstacle or sound.
SILKS	A jacket worn by jockeys designating the owner of the horse.
SIRE	The father of a horse.
SIT CHILLY	When a jockey sits on a horse very calmly and waits to make a move at the desired time.
SIX FURLONGS	¾ of a mile, 1320 yards, 3960 feet.
SIXTEENTH	One sixteenth of a mile, 110 yards, 330 feet.
SKINNED TRACK	A dirt racing strip as opposed to a grass (turf) course.
SLEEPER	A horse that suddenly perks up and runs a surprisingly strong race.
SLOPPY TRACK	A track that is firm underneath but with puddles of water on top.
SLOT	The horses post position in a race.

SLOW TRACK	A track that is drying out but not yet "GOOD".
SNATCH UP	When a jockey pulls a horse up sharply, usually because he is cut off by another horse.
SNIP	A small patch of white hair on the tip of the nose of a horse.
SOCKS	The white markings on a horse's legs below the fetlocks.
SOLID HORSE	A horse that is considered a contender.
SOPHMORES	Three year old horses, in their second year of racing.
SORE	A horse sensitive to pain from pressure. A horse that is lame or tender.
SOUND	A horse that is not lame, tender, or injured in any way.
SOUPY	A term sometimes used to describe a sloppy track.
SPEED DUEL	When two or more horses battle early in the race to get the lead.

SPEED HANDICAPPERS	Those that believe a horse's ability can be measured by how fast it runs. They use different calculations to translate a horse's ability into a number. The highest number being the superior horse.
SPEED HORSE	A horse that breaks fast from the gates and usually goes to the front to set the pace for the other horses in the race.
SPEED RATING	Indicates how a horse's time compares with the track record. A speed rating of 100 is a track record.
SPEED RIDER	A jockey who has the ability to consistently get a horse out of the gates fast, usually breaking on top, which gives a speed horse a definate advantage.
SPEEDY CUT	An injury to the rear of a horse's front leg, just above the hoof, caused by being struck with one of the hind feet, while racing.
SPILL	An accident involving one or more horses and jockeys.
SPINNING OUT OF THE TURN	A term used by track announcer Phil Georgeff describing the horses as they complete the final stretch turn.
SPIT BOX	The place where specimens are taken to determine if a horse is drugged.

SPLINT   A small round bony enlargement located between the splint bone and cannon bone.

SPOT BETTOR   A bettor who bets only occasionally; when he believes that he has a certain edge in his favor.

SPRINT   A race that is less than a mile distance.

SPRINTER   A horse who has a lot of speed over a short distance but is seldom able to maintain that speed over a long distance.

SPUR   A metal device that is strapped on to a riders boot to urge a horse to run faster.

STABLE   A building where horses are housed; also a collection of race horses, such as a racing stable.

STABLE NAME   An assumed name or farm name, such as The Triple B Farms, under which a person or persons, race horses. The identity of the actual owners can be kept confidential to everyone but the registering authority.

STAKE   A reward or gratuity given to a jockey, trainer, groom or other stable employees as a bonus to celebrate the winning of a race.

STAKE HORSE   A horse that usually races in stake races.

145

STAKE RACE	A race in which the purse is made up of fee's put up by the owners of the horses in the race. The race track will usually place additional money in the purse. A stakes race usually has a collection of the best horses. There are different grades of stake races, the Triple Crown races are among those considered as Grade One Stakes.
STALE	Off form. A horse not running up to its potential.
STALL	A compartment in a stable in which the horse lives.
STALLION	An un-altered male horse. A horse that has not been castrated.
STALL WALKER	A horse that is nervous and moves around in it's stall and does not rest.
STAND UP	When a jockey stands errect in his stirrups either because he snatches up the horse or at the end of the race. Standing up gives the jockey the leverage that is necessary to try to stop or slow down a horse, although some horses must be stopped by the outrider at the end of the race.
STANDS	Refers to a stallion standing at stud.

STANDS	Sometimes used in referring to the grand stands.
STAR	A small patch of white hair on a horses head.
STARTER	The Official who is responsible for overseeing the loading of the starting gates and insuring that all horses get an equal start in the race. He is also the official who presses the button that opens the starting gates at the start of the race.
STARTER	A horse that breaks from the starting gates, is considered a starter even if it doesn't finish the race.
STARTERS LIST	A list of horses that are required to be schooled in the starting gates before they are eligible to race, usually because of their misbehavior in the gates during the start of a race.
STARTING BELL	The bell that rings signifying the start of the race. Also called the off bell and the closing bell because it signifies the closing of wagering.
STARTING GATE	A device with partitions for horses in which they are confined until the Starter opens the doors in front of them, thus starting the race.

147

STATE BRED   A horse that is bred in the State in which it is racing.

STAYER   A stout-hearted horse, one that does not quit.

STAY OFF THE PACE   When a jockey is told to lag behind the leaders in a race.

STEADIED   A term used to describe altering the speed of a horse in a race. It is less severe to steady a horse than to check it or take up the horse.

STEAL A RACE   When a trainer tries to win a race by entering a horse in a race where the other horses are far inferior.

STEWARDS   There are usually three Stewards that supervise a race meeting. They are judges of all matters concerning the conduct of the race meeting.

STEWARDS LIST   A list of horses that either act up in the paddock, or run poorly in a race. A horse must be taken off the list before it is allowed to race.

STICK   A whip or crop used by a jockey.

STICKERS   Calks on a horse's shoes which give it better traction in the mud.

STIFF	To deliberately prevent a horse from winning.
STIFLE OUT	The condition where the patella, a part of the stiffle joint, becomes dislocated.
STIRRUP	A metal loop suspended from the saddle of a horse to support a jockey's foot. Also called Irons.
STIRRUP LEATHERS	The adjustable strap that attaches the stirrup irons to the saddle.
STIRRUP STOCKINGS	When the legs of the horse are white below the knees.
STOOPER	An individual who makes money by picking up discarded winning pari-mutual tickets at the track. Also called a FLIPPER.
STOPPING THE TIMER	Finishing the race; the time stops when the race is over.
STOP WATCH	In horse racing it is a watch which registers time in fifths of a second and starts and stops by pressing a button.
STRAIGHT	When a bettor bets on a horse to WIN a race, rather than PLACE or SHOW.
STRAW	A bedding used in a horse's stall.

STRETCH	The straightaway portion of the race track that ends at the finish line.
STRETCH CALL	The call of the race by the announcer, as the horses are racing in the stretch.
STRETCH KICK	A final effort that a horse exerts in the stretch to try to win a race.
STRETCH RUNNER	A horse known to start slowly but to finish strong.
STRETCH TURN	The bend of track coming into the homestretch.
STRIDE	The distance between a horse's steps, a manner of going.
STRING	A group of race horses owned by one stable or trained by one trainer.
STRIPE	A narrow mark of white that runs down the horse's face to the bridge of the nose or below.
STUD	A male horse used for breeding. A term also used for stallion.
STUD BOOK	The registry and record of the breeding of Thoroughbreds.
STUD FARM	A farm that houses stallions that are used for breeding purposes.

150

STUD FEE The price that is charged to the owner of a mare by the stallion owner, for the breeding services of the stallion.

SUBSCRIPTION The fee paid by owners to nominate a horse for a race and to maintain eligibility for it.

SUBSTITUTE RACE A race that is run in case a regularly scheduled race doesn't fill or is canceled.

SUCKLING A baby horse that is still nursing.

SULK This is when a horse refuses to extend itself.

SURCINGLE A wide band with a buckle that is used to keep a horse blanket in place.

SUSPEND To revolk the license of any licensed track personnel such as jockey, trainer, owner, groom, hot-walker, etc. for an infraction of the rules. These suspensions can range from days, to a lifetime, depending on the violation.

SWAYBACK A horse with a dipped backbone.

SWEAT BOX The steam room that the jockeys use to sweat off unwanted pounds, also called the HOT BOX, or the BOX.

SWEAT SCRAPER	A thin aluminum curved blade about twelve inches long used to scrape sweat and excess water off a horse.
SWEEP SIX	A wager where the bettor must pick the winners of six consecutive races to collect the jackpot, which is normally huge.
SWIMMING	Many trainers swim their horses to condition them for racing.
SWIPE	A groom.
SWITCH STICKS	This is when a jockey changes hands with the whip, while in race.
SYSTEM	A procedure that some handicappers use as a shortcut to finding potential winners or winning bets.
TACK	The gear used in equipping a horse, which includes a saddle, briddle, halter, etc.
TACK ROOM	A room in the stable area that is used to store tack and is often used by stable employees to live and sleep in.
TAG	The claiming price that is established for a horse by the owner or trainer.
TAIL END	The horse that is last in the race is said to be on the tail end.

152

TAKE (Mutuel) The commission deducted from the mutuel pool which is shared by the track and the state in which the race is in.

TAKE BACK When a jockey holds a horse back at the start of a race to reserve the horse's strength for a later time in the race; letting other horses go by.

TAKE HOLD This is when a jockey restrains a horse from running all out.

TAKEN DOWN When a horse finishes a race in either of the first four places which is shown on the board, and in the process of the race, fouls another horse, it is TAKEN DOWN off the board, disqualified and placed accordingly, before the race is declared "OFFICIAL".

TAKE OFF When a jockey refuses to ride the mounts that he is scheduled to ride for the day. Either the jockey is sick or he feels the horse isn't sound.

TAKE UP When a jockey pulls the horse up sharply to avoid getting into trouble with another horse during the race.

TAKE YOUR NUMBER DOWN It is when a horse finishes a race in one of the first four positions and its number is placed on the tote board, and then because of an inquiry the horse is disqualified and it's number is taken down.

153

TATTOO	A permanent number stamped in a horses lip to identify him.
TELE-TRACK	Off track betting facility using a large TV screen to show actual races.
TELLER	The person who accepts the bets at the pari-mutuel windows.
TEMPERATURE	The normal temperature of a horse is 100.5ºF.
TESTED	When another horse comes up to challenge the leader in a race, and makes him go all out to win.
THREE-EIGHTH POLE	A green and white pole inside the inside rail three-eighth of mile from the finish line.
THREE-QUARTERS POLE	A red and white pole inside the inside rail three-quarters of a mile from the finish line.
THOROUGH-BRED	Refers to the Thoroughbred Race Horse whose ancestry may be traced in the direct male line to one of three stallions, The Byerly Turk, The Darley Arabian, or The Godolphin Barb.

THOROUGH-BRED RECORD The oldest racing bloodstock journal in the United States, which was founded in 1875. A weekly magazine concerned mainly with owner, trainers and others involved with Thoroughbred racing.

THRUSH An inflammation of the lower structure of the frog of the horse's hoof. A moist foul smelling, dark rot found in the frog of the foot. Probably the most common foot ailment.

TICKET The pari-mutuel ticket which is the receipt of a bet.

TIGHT This is when a horse is in good condition and ready to race.

TIP A piece of private or secret information to be considered in betting.

TIP SHEET A leaflet or sheet sold, at or near the track, which list the publishers selections or what he considers the best bets of the day.

TIPSTER Same as tout; a person who gives information on betting a horse.

TONGUE STRAP A strap or piece of material used to tie down a horses tongue to prevent it from choking on it in a race.

TOP FORM   When a horse is in top racing condition.

TOP LINE   The breeding on the sires side, also called TOP SIDE.

TOP SIDE   A horses breeding ancestry on the sire's side; also called TOP LINE.

TOP WEIGHT   The highest poundage assigned to the horse.

TOTALIZATOR   An intricate machine which handles betting tickets, records totals bet on each race, totals bets on each horse, shows the odds to WIN on each horse, and the payoff after the race. It also displays all the information.

TOTE BOARD   The sign that displays the information for the totalizator.

TOUT   To give information on betting a horse.

TOUT (A)   A person who gives information on betting a horse.

TOUT SHEET   A paper sold with horse racing information and selections.

T.R.A.   Thoroughbred Racing Association. An organization consisting of race track management and functions along the line of a trade association.

TRACK	An oval surface used to hold a race on.
TRACK BIAS	When a track is faster at certain parts and favors the horses running there. If the rail is the fastest part of the track; then the horse with early speed or an inside post position is favored. Each racing strip is different. Sometimes the rail is the deepest and slowest part of the track.
TRACK CHEMIST	An official that is assigned the task of analyzing urine, saliva and blood samples after a race to insure that they are free from any illegal drugs.
TRACK CONDITION	A term used to describe the overall surface of the racing strip. Fast, Slow, Muddy, etc.
TRACK KITCHEN	A restaurant on the backstretch for horsemen and other track personnel.
TRACK ODDS	The odds that are posted on the tote board after all bets are totalled and the race is started, that determines the prices to be paid at the race track on all wagers.
TRACK RECORD	The fastest time recorded in a race for a certain distance over a particular course.

TRACK VARIANT	It indicates whether a track was faster or slower than normal on a certain day, also the quality of horses running that day.
TRAIL	When a horse finishes behind the rest of the field.
TRAINER	The person who is in charge of caring for, conditioning and entering a horse in a race. The trainer is responsible for all the horses and employees under his control at all times while on the race track.
TRAINERS AUTHORIZED AGENT	The person authorized by the trainer to represent him on racing matters.
TRAINING TRACK	An auxiliary race track that is used for workouts and schooling.
TRI-FECTA	A race where the bettor must pick the first, second and third place horses, in the exact order of finish to win.
TRIPLE	When a jockey or trainer wins three races in one day: also refers to Trifecta; a race where the bettor must pick the first, second, and third place horses, in the exact order of finish to win.

TRIPLE CROWN   The Triple Crown consist of three impor-
tant races for 3 year olds. In
Thoroughbred racing the three races
comprising the Triple Crown are the
Kentucky Derby, the Preakness Stakes
and the Belmont Stakes. In Britain, the
Triple Crown consist of the Derby, the
Two Thousand Guineas and the St.
Leger. In the U.S. there is also a
Thoroughbred Triple Crown for fillies.
The three races are the Acorn, the
Mother Goose Stakes and the Coaching
Club American Oaks.

T.R.P.B.   Thoroughbred Racing Protective Bureau.
It is a national investigative organization
that is maintained by the Thoroughbred
Racing Association.

TUBE WORM   It is when a veterinarian puts a long tube
down the nostril of a horse and pumps
a worming medicine into it. Many
horsemen feel that this is the best way
to worm a horse.

TURF ACCOUNTANT   A book maker licensed to take bets on
horse races in Great Britain.

TURF COURSE   A racing course on the grass.

TWITCH   A device which is a handle with a rope
or chain loop at one end, which is put
around the horse's nose and upper lip to
help control it.

159

TWO MINUTE LICK	A pace used in exercising a horse. Galloping one mile in two minutes.
UNCOCKING THE STICK	A jockey switches the position of his whip after breaking from the starting gate, which is called UNCOCKING THE STICK.
UNDER A DRIVE	When a horse is under pressure to exert a maximum effort by it's jockey.
UNDER CONTRACT	A rider or trainee with an agreement signed for a specified time with an owner.
UNDER PUNISHMENT	When a horse is whipped and pushed on during a race.
UNDER WRAPS	This is when a horse is under a stout restraint in a race or workout.
UNFIT	A horse that is not in top racing condition, and usually tires before the end of the race.
UNPLACED	A horse that finished a race in any position other than the first three positions. WIN, PLACE, or SHOW.
UNRACED	A horse that has not started in an official race.
UNSEATED	When a rider has fallen off a horse.

UNSOUND	A horse that is lame or injured.
UNTRIED	A horse that has never been raced or (in breeding) a horse that has never been bred.
UNWIND	To gradually withdraw a horse from training.
UP	The jockey that is riding, or is assigned to ride, a certain horse.
UP THE TRACK	A horse that finished a race far behind the leaders.
URINALYSIS	A laboratory test of urine to determine if a horse is drugged.
USED UP	A horse that stopped running before the end of the race, lacking stamina.
VALET	A person who attends to a jockey and keeps the equipment in order. He is also required to help saddle the horse in the paddock.
VAN	A truck or trailer used to transport horses.
VETERINARIAN	A horse or animal doctor.

VETS LIST	A list of horses which have either bled or pulled up in a race becasue of soreness or injury. An injured or unsound horse put on this list must be approved by the Track Veterinarian before it is able to race.
VICE	A bad habit that a horse may have, such as biting, kicking, striking, rearing, etc.
WAGER	Money risked or staked on an uncertain event, also called a bet.
WALK HOTS	To walk a horse until it cools off after a race or workout.
WALKOVER	A race, which scratches down to only one horse, who usually just gallops the distance of the race.
WALL OF THE FOOT	The part of the hoof that is visible when the foot is placed flat on the ground.
WARM UP	Galloping a horse on the way to the starting gate.
WASH OUT	A horse breaking out in a nervous sweat before the start of the race.
WASHY	Another term used for a horse that is washed out.

162

WAY OF GOING The way in which a horse moves, usually referring to a horse moving in an unnatural manner.

WEAN (TO) To separate a foal from its mother.

WEANLING A baby horse that is not yet one year old, from the time of foaling until the first of January, and is separated from its mother.

WEAVE Said of a horse that runs in a staggering manner going right and left rather than in a straight line.

WEBBING A material used on the front of the stall as a barrier to keep a horse in.

WEIGH-IN The official weighing of a jockey and his saddle and equipment after a race.

WEIGHT ALLOWANCES A concession of weights to be carried by a horse in a race. Such as an apprentice jockey allowance or a sex allowance, etc.

WEIGHT FOR AGE A fixed scale of weight to be carried by horses according to age, sex, distance of race, and season of year.

WHEEL A horse that veers sharply to the right or left trying to turn in an opposite direction.

163

WHEEL (betting)	To bet one horse in a combination with all the other horses in a gimmick race.
WHISTLING	A result of overstraining a horse's lungs and respiratory muscles.
WHIP	A crop or stick the jockeys use to urge a horse in a race.
WHOLE HORSE	A horse that has not been castrated.
WIDE	Toward the outside of the racing surface farthest from the rail.
WIN	When placing a bet on a horse to WIN, you are betting that the horse finishes the race in FIRST PLACE. The horse must WIN the race in order for you to collect your bet.
WIN BET	A wager that a horse will finish in FIRST PLACE in a race. The horse must finish in FIRST PLACE in order to collect money on a WIN bet.
WINDED	A horse breathing with difficulty after a race or workout.
WINDOWS	Where a person places his bets at the race track.
WINDSUCKER	A horse that places his upper incisor teeth on a ledge, presses down, and swallows air at the same time.

WINNER	The horse whose nose reaches the wire first. A horse shall not be considered the winner until the race is declared "OFFICIAL". If there is a dead heat for First Place, both horses shall be considered WINNERS.
WINNER CIRCLE	The place where the jockey brings the horse after winning a race, to weight in and get pictures taken.
WIN MONEY	The money or portion of the purse that an owner of a horse would receive because the horse finished in First Place. Is is also the payoff on a Win bet.
WINNER TAKES ALL	The winner of the race wins the entire purse.
WIN POOL	The total amount of money wagered to WIN on a particular race, after all commissions and taxes are deducted.
WINTER BOOK	It is when a bookmaker offers odds in the winter, on a race or races to be held the following summer. The odds are given on all qualified entries and the bettors lose their money if the horse does not compete in the race.
WIRE	The finish line.
WIRE TO WIRE	When the horse takes the lead from the start of the race and never relinquishes it.

165

WITHDRAW   To scratch a horse from a race.

WITHERS   The highest part of a horses back at the base of the neck.

WOLF TEETH   Extra teeth found just forward from the first upper molar. They must be removed.

WOOD (THE)   A term referring to the rail, which originally was made of wood.

WORK   To exercise a horse as if it were in a race. A workout.

WORK A HORSE   To exercise a horse at a fast pace, as in a race.

WORK IN COMPANY   When two or more horses are exercised together.

WORKOUT   To exercise a horse at a fast pace. Same as work a horse.

WOUND TIGHT   A horse that is feeling good and is in good racing condition.

WRONG WAY   Going around the track clockwise, or in the opposite direction as in a race.

YEARLING   A horse one year old, dating from January 1 of the year of foaling.

YEARLING SALE   An auction which is conducted to handle yearlings.

SATISFACTION GUARANTEED

ORDER FORM

TO: **BIG HOUSE PUBLISHING**
P.O. Box 202
Steger, Illinois 60475
(312) 758-8786

Please send _____ copies of ***Glossary of Thoroughbred Racing,***
By Frank M. Briggs, Sr.

Hard Cover	$14.95
Soft Cover 6 x 9	$9.95

Please send _____ copies of ***Becoming A Jockey,*** A Booklet
By Eddie Roberts

Paperback	$3.95

Please add sales tax of 7% ($1.05 for Hard Cover .70 for Soft Cover
to all books shipped to Illinois Addresses)

Name _____

Address _____

City / State / Zip _____

Shipping:

          ☐ Book Rate   1.00 per book

          ☐ Air Mail   3.00 per book

L.C.	86-070592	
ISBN	0-937529-04-4	Hardcover
ISBN	0-937529-03-6	Softcover

I understand that I may return the book(s) within
30 days for a full refund--for any reason, no
questions asked.

SATISFACTION GUARANTEED
ORDER FORM
TO: BIG HOUSE PUBLISHING
P.O. Box 202
Steger, Illinois 60475
(312) 758-8786

Please send _____ copies of *Glossary of Thoroughbred Racing,*
By Frank M. Briggs, Sr.

Hard Cover $14.95
Soft Cover   6 x 9 $9.95

Please send _____ copies of *Becoming A Jockey,* A Booklet
By Eddie Roberts

Paperback $3.95

Please add sales tax of 7% ($1.05 for Hard Cover .70 for Soft Cover
to all books shipped to Illinois Addresses)

Name _____

Address _____

City / State / Zip _____

Shipping:

☐ Book Rate   1.00 per book

☐ Air Mail   3.00 per book

L.C.   86-070592
ISBN   0-937529-04-4   Hardcover
ISBN   0-937529-03-6   Softcover

I understand that I may return the book(s) within
30 days for a full refund--for any reason, no
questions asked.

SATISFACTION GUARANTEED

ORDER FORM

TO: BIG HOUSE PUBLISHING

P.O. Box 202
Steger, Illinois 60475
(312) 758-8786

Please send _____ copies of *Glossary of Thoroughbred Racing,*
By Frank M. Briggs, Sr.

Hard Cover $14.95
Soft Cover   6 x 9 $9.95

Please send _____ copies of *Becoming A Jockey,* A Booklet
By Eddie Roberts

Paperback $3.95

Please add sales tax of 7% ($1.05 for Hard Cover .70 for Soft Cover
to all books shipped to Illinois Addresses)

Name _____

Address _____

City / State / Zip _____

Shipping:

☐ Book Rate   1.00 per book

☐ Air Mail   3.00 per book

L.C.   86-070592
ISBN   0-937529-04-4   Hardcover
ISBN   0-937529-03-6   Softcover

I understand that I may return the book(s) within
30 days for a full refund--for any reason, no
questions asked.

SATISFACTION GUARANTEED

ORDER FORM

TO: BIG HOUSE PUBLISHING
P.O. Box 202
Steger, Illinois 60475
(312) 758-8786

Please send _____ copies of *Glossary of Thoroughbred Racing,*
By Frank M. Briggs, Sr.

Hard Cover	$14.95
Soft Cover 6 x 9	$9.95

Please send _____ copies of *Becoming A Jockey,* A Booklet
By Eddie Roberts

Paperback	$3.95

Please add sales tax of 7% ($1.05 for Hard Cover .70 for Soft Cover
to all books shipped to Illinois Addresses)

Name _____

Address _____

City / State / Zip _____

Shipping:

☐ Book Rate   1.00 per book

☐ Air Mail   3.00 per book

L.C.	86-070592	
ISBN	0-937529-04-4	Hardcover
ISBN	0-937529-03-6	Softcover

I understand that I may return the book(s) within
30 days for a full refund--for any reason, no
questions asked.